AF496475

THE BOOK OF WESTON-SUPER-MARE

COVER: Weston-super-Mare: a 19th century panorama.

'An irregularly-built, straggling group of houses . . . a grand sweep of sands . . . and, before you — the Sea! Rather brown-coloured . . . but still the sea. I . . . advise you to pack up your traps for Weston-super-Mare, which you may rely upon liking.' *(Illustrated Midland News,* 20 November, 1869.)

THE BOOK OF WESTON -SUPER- MARE

THE STORY OF THE TOWN'S PAST

BY

BRYAN J. H. BROWN BSc PhD

AND

JOHN LOOSLEY ALA

BARRACUDA BOOKS LIMITED
BUCKINGHAM, ENGLAND
MCMLXXIX

PUBLISHED BY BARRACUDA BOOKS LIMITED

BUCKINGHAM, ENGLAND

AND PRINTED BY

FRANK ROOK LIMITED

TOWER BRIDGE ROAD

LONDON SE1

BOUND BY

BOOKBINDERS OF LONDON LIMITED

LONDON N5

JACKET PRINTED BY

WHITE CRESCENT PRESS LIMITED

LUTON, ENGLAND

LITHOGRAPHY BY

SOUTH MIDLANDS LITHO PLATES LIMITED

LUTON, ENGLAND

DISPLAY TYPE SET IN

MONOTYPE BASKERVILLE SERIES 169

BY SOUTH BUCKS TYPESETTERS LIMITED

BEACONSFIELD, ENGLAND

TEXT SET IN 12/14PT BASKERVILLE

BY BEAVER REPROGRAPHICS LIMITED

BUSHEY, ENGLAND

ISBN 0 86023 114 3

Contents

Acknowledgements

We would like to place on record our sincere thanks to all the individuals and institutions whose help has made the publication of this volume possible. Dr Brown's original research, undertaken at the University of Bath with the help of a Social Science Research Council Studentship, owed much to the guiding hand of Dr R. A. Buchanan, and was only made possible by the continuing and generous support of his parents. During that period (1968-1971) the Weston-super-Mare Library and Museum, then under the direction of G. P. Rye, also provided constant assistance. The staffs of the Somerset Record Office, the Bristol Reference Library and several of the Departments of the former Weston-super-Mare Corporation are also thanked for their help then, while access to the Smyth-Pigott papers was kindly arranged by Messrs J. Hodge and Co. The subsequent compilation of the present volume has been made possible by the generous co-operation of the Avon County Library Service and the Director of Libraries, R. E. Grimshaw, to whom our sincere thanks are due for permission to reproduce most of the illustrations. We are especially grateful to Jane Evans of Woodspring Museum for her help and encouragement during the compilation of the text, and for permission to reproduce illustrations from the Museum collection. Particular appreciation is due to the Avon County Library Service, Weston-super-Mare Library staff, Jane Evans of Woodspring and the Woodspring District Council for invaluable help with the essential subscription facility.

We are also pleased to acknowledge the help of Harry King and George Dickason of the Publicity and Public Relations Department of Woodspring District Council and Basil Flavell and Tony Blizzard of the Leisure Services Department of Woodspring District Council.

Thanks are due to Martin Taylor of the Weston-super-Mare Civic Society for the assistance so willingly given.

David Tomalin of Carisbrooke Castle Museum and John White of West Air Photography have generously given permission for us to reproduce illustrations.

Our especial thanks are due to Stella Hill for typing much of the material and for great encouragement and to Peter Loosley for his assistance with research.

Last, but by no means least, our thanks are extended to Susan Brown, who not only typed the text but has so skillfully undertaken the drawing of all the maps and diagrams.

Most illustrations in this book are reproduced by kind permission of the Director of Libraries for the County of Avon and are from the collection at the Central Library, Weston-super-Mare.

Other illustrations are kindly supplied by Woodspring Museum, Burlington Street, W.s.M. — WM; West Air Photography, Cecil Road, W.s.M. — WAP.

Foreword

by G. P. Rye, FLA, Borough Librarian and Curator 1951-1974

To have an interest in the history of one's county, town or parish and to want to know more is no new phenomenon, and we are indebted to countless men and women who have during the past three or more centuries painstakingly sought out details of their localities. Within the last fifty years and particularly within the last twenty, the study of local history has become widespread and books and pamphlets on local topics are avidly read by thousands.

Weston-super-Mare has been fortunate in that many persons have recorded their memories or sought out information about the town. The contributions of Ernest Baker, Edwin Knight and the two brothers Ronald and John Bailey have been outstanding and Edwin Knight's book *The Seaboard of Mendip*, published in 1902, has been the principal account of the town and the surrounding villages. Since then archaeological and social studies have been taking place and these have deepened our knowledge and understanding of the area.

Earlier local studies tended to be accumulations of facts and as such they are invaluable: thus it is possible to know when a bridge was built or a terrace of houses erected. What is not so easily discovered is why the building took place. Contemporary local historians are seeking more and more to try and answer the question 'why' in addition to just discovering 'when' and 'what'.

Dr Brown, for his thesis on the coastal resorts of the Severn Estuary, was concerned with the reasons for their origins and subsequent development. First his researches were concerned with the basic data — the what and when, and thus it was that he turned to John Loosley and the local history collection in the Weston-super-Mare Public Library. The result was a pioneering study of Weston-super-Mare relating the development of the town to the national economy of the country.

Those researches aroused his interest in the town and particularly in its industrial enterprises. Linking these with John Loosley's intimate knowledge of the available local material, together they have given us the up-to-date account of the town which has been long overdue. The text and illustrations combine to provide a mine of information and will, I hope, encourage many to carry out further research on items of particular personal interest. Local history is constantly being made and records of contemporary events are as important as those of the past so the story does not stop with this publication.

The Book of Weston-super-Mare will, I hope, be treasured by all who have a love for the town and be a source of great pleasure to resident and visitor alike. May it encourage them to look at the town with new eyes.

Geof. Rye.

The spirit of Weston — in 1896: family elegance and the famous Weston donkey cart.

Mrs Piozzi's Letter

Weston-super-Mare 27 : Aug : 1819.

I feel delighted Dear Sir that you have not forgotten me; some Ladies that I met upon the Sands last night said Sir James Fellowes had mention'd my Name at Gay and fashionable Bognor. This little Place is neither gay nor fashionable yet full as an Egg, insipid as the White on't and dear as an Egg o' Penny. I enquir'd for Books, there were but Two in the Town was the reply . . . a Bible and a Paradise Lost. . . . They were the best however. No Market . . . but I dont care about that.

. . . The Breezes here are most Salubrious; no Land nearer than North America, when we look down the Channel: and tis said that Sebastian Cabot used to stand where I sit now & meditate his future Discoveries of Newfoundland. Who would be living at Bath now? The Bottom of the Town a Stewpot, the top a Gridiron, and London in a State of Defence or Preparation for Attack or some strange Situation while poor little Weston is free from Alarms . . .

We have swarms of Babies here, and some bathe good humouredly enough while others scream and shriek as if they were going to Execution. . . .

I am going on a Water Party next Monday with a very agreeable Young Man, Mr Rogers: There are few People here that I know, one Lady however challenged me as an Acquaintance of her Brothers—just 70 Years ago when he was a little Boy at Weston School and used to come home for Holydays with Sir Robert Salusbury Cotton Father of this Lord Combermere to our House in Jermyn Street, now part of Blake's Hotel.

Adieu Dear Sir— portez vous bien: present me to Lady Fellowes, and tell your children they have an humble & an attached Servt. in

H: L: PIOZZI.

Sir James Fellowes,
Bognor Rocks, Sussex.

Dedication

To Susan and Paddy

ABOVE: Mammoth's tooth found at Southside. (WM)
LEFT & RIGHT: stone axes from Worlebury (WM)
and CENTRE: a Roman brooch found at the site of the new Technical College. (WM)

Weston-propre-Worle

The town of Weston-super-Mare, which is now part of the District of Woodspring in Avon County, stretches along part of the eastern shore of the lower Severn Estuary, and dominates the lowland long known as the North Marsh of Somerset. During the past two centuries it has grown from almost total obscurity to become one of the leading seaside resorts of the United Kingdom, but it has also developed as an industrial, service and residential town offering a healthy and enjoyable environment for more than 50,000 Westonians. The limits of Weston are relatively easily defined, for the town is isolated by lowland moor and the river Banwell on the north-east, and by the westernmost extension of the Mendip Hills to the south. However, a wider area of both South Avon and North Somerset look to the town for shopping, employment and entertainment, while holiday visitors come from all parts of the country and abroad.

Weston's landscape is one of contrasts. Much of the town is built on flat low lying land which is composed of alluvium, which consists of blue muds, silty sands and small quantities of peat. This land never rises above 20ft O.D., but in places the alluvium is over 90ft deep. It was formed during a long period when the shallow estuarine seas lay higher than they do today, a fact also attested to by the presence on all the coastal headlands of 'raised beach' deposits at between 24 and 50ft above present sea level. Some of the alluvial clays have proved suitable for pottery and brick making, and provided the basis for one of the town's former major industries. Rising abruptly from the low plain, and creating impressive and dominating features in the otherwise flat landscape, are the three east-west ridge hills of Worlebury, Brean Down and Middle Hope. These are composed of hard carboniferous limestone, which was laid down some 250 million years ago on the bed of a shallow warm sea, and geologically are a part of the nearby Mendip Hills. The great earth movements of the Hercynian mountain-building period have folded the rock to form the present hills, and there is evidence of volcanic activity associated with this process which produced localised lavas and faulting. In the geologically recent past these hills were islands, separated from Mendip by the shallow seas covering the lower ground, and were only linked to the mainland as a result of falling sea level combined with the formation of sand spits and gradual accumulation of alluvium. Surrounding each of the limestone ridges is a thin band of dolomitic conglomerate and Keuper marl, the former indicating that the hills were already in existence and being eroded some 225 million years ago. These provide small areas of rather better quality land above the level of flooding and contrast with the steep slopes and relatively poor soils which are developed on the limestone itself.

Present day Weston is essentially a 19th century town, and until mediaeval times was little more than a swamp. Evidence of early man is scant, and limited to the higher land. The animals of the Ice Age have left evidence of their presence in the form of some teeth preserved in fissures in several local quarries however, providing illustrations of a time when rhinoceros, mammoth and giant Irish deer roamed on Worle Hill. Flints from the Old Stone Age have been found in caves at Uphill, but the first real evidence of men on Worlebury did not come until the New Stone Age. Then the hilltop was favoured for occupation and some settlement continued in the Bronze Age, as is evident from bronze implements which were found on the hill and burial urns dug up in Ashcombe cemetery.

In the Iron Age the hill-top was settled, and a large hill-fort was constructed, the remains of which can still be seen clearly today. It was one of a series of such forts along the north edge of Mendip, and was second only in size to that at Dolebury. The Iron Age settlers were obviously impressed by the fine views and easily defended position which Worlebury offered, and also by a supply of fresh water at Spring Cove and a large area of land suitable for cultivation. The great ramparts, which date from the later Iron Age, take in more than ten acres, and many people could have lived in the fort itself. However many more also lived lower down the slopes of the hill, as evidenced by pit burials found in Grove Park and Stafford Place. The fort must have acted as a refuge for people in times of trouble, and large quantities of slingstone (natural beach pebbles) have been found. Inside the fort many pits 5 to 6ft deep and 6ft across have been found, and it is assumed that these were for the storage of grain and later for rubbish. A thatch roof was normally put over the top of them to stop the penetration of rain.

During the 1st century AD the fort was attacked, possibly by the Romans, and life on Worlebury came to a dramatic and tragic end. Bodies were flung into the pits, and some of these had been severely wounded, with one skull showing seven sword cuts. After this episode the fort was abandoned for some time, and in the Romano-British period the local inhabitants must have contented themselves with farming on the lower slopes in the Park Place/Royal Crescent area and further along the hill, as is shown by the pottery and coins which were found at Milton around Roslyn Avenue.

With the coming of the Normans in 1066 and the compilation of the Domesday record in 1086 we have what must be a record of the local hamlets which had become established either in this period of Roman occupation or during the ensuing Dark Ages. In fact the Domesday record does not mention Weston-super-Mare by name, although there is reason to suppose that a rudimentary fishing hamlet was then in existence below the present site of the Parish Church, but the Weston area was well represented, and obviously well established. Weston itself was apparently included in the manor of *Aisecome* (Ashcombe), while there are also entries for *Worspring* (Woodspring), *Chiwestock* (Kewstoke), Worle, *Middeltone* (Milton), and *Opopille* (Uphill). Together these manors occupied all of the easily cultivable land in the district, and probably used both the bare limestone hills and the marshy lowland for pasture. All the manors were in the Hundred of Winterstoke, although there is now no trace of the village of that name, which is thought to have been in the Banwell area.

Of the Weston area manors, Worle appears to have been the most important, certainly on financial grounds. It was worth 7 pounds at the time of the survey, although 10 pounds immediately before the Norman invasion, perhaps indicating some destruction and problems during the fighting and takeover by King William. However, in 1086 the manor was held by Walter de Dowai from the King, and it included land for 15 ploughs and 50 acres of meadow together with one riding horse, 24 beasts (cattle), 18 swine and 60 sheep. Local ownership was varied, Herluin holding Ashcombe from the Bishop of Coutances, who also owned Kewstoke, William de Faleise holding Woodspring and four knights (*milites*) holding Uphill from its owner Serlo de Burci. Walter de Dowai also held Milton which he leased to one Richard whose surname is not recorded. This was by far the least valuable manor, only worth 25 shillings. The ownership of all the manors had changed following the invasion as property was distributed to William's followers, but the working population would have remained, organised under the Norman feudal system.

Of Weston itself there was no mention however, and no written reference to the place exists until an entry in the *Registers* of the Dean and Chapter of Wells for 1226 which set out an ordinance of Bishop Jocelin about the various dues to be rendered to the Treasurer of Wells. Among these is 'Of the Rector of Weston, 100 lb of wax whereof he shall find the sub Treasurer in the Church of St Andrew, and he shall receive yearly 11s and puture.' Clearly the Church at Weston was already established by that date, and must have been constructed to serve an existing settlement. Even in the Worlebury excavations the presence of limpet shells indicates the use of the sea as a food resource, and it seems most likely that Weston's origin is connected with the development of fishing on the Ashcombe manor, and that its early inhabitants combined fishing and farming for their livelihood. The number of residents must have been sufficient to warrant the building of a church some time during the 12th or early 13th centuries, and since there is no record of a church at Ashcombe itself presumably no settlement of substance had developed around the manor farm.

Weston's present name appears to have been the result of clerical strivings to differentiate between the many Westons in the Somerset area. Several variants were used before the present one, the first being Weston-propre-Worle in 1234, then by 1311 Weston-juxta-Worle, Weston-juxta-Mare, Weston-upon-More, and finally Weston-super-Mare in the Bath and Wells *Register* for 1348. This later tag, denoting a seaside location, seems to have stuck, and has perhaps been an asset to more recent developers of the town as a dignified and unique placename. Thus by the 14th century Weston-super-Mare had become clearly established, and was a manor in its own right, although for long tied to Ashcombe by common ownership.

Following the Norman conquest one further and significant change in the settlement pattern of the Weston area was to take place, that being the transformation of *Worspring*. From the Domesday survey it is clear that the settlement at *Worspring*, (subsequently Woodspring) was substantial, being of a similar value to Ashcombe and Uphill. The remains of a 'motte' or small castle mound, and evidence of field systems on Middle Hope, suggest a substantial manor house and village. Of this today there is no trace however, and its subsequent disappearance is presumably closely linked with the establishment of the Worspring Priory.

The Priory, whose inmates were Victorine canons who followed the Augustinian rule and were connected with the larger house of Austin canons in Bristol, was founded about 1210 by William de Courteney, a grandson of Reginald Fitz Urse of Williton, one of the four knights who murdered Thomas Becket, Archbishop of Canterbury, in Canterbury Cathedral on 29 December 1170. There is no surviving charter of foundation, but the expressed object was 'the establishment here of ecclesiastics who should maintain constant prayers for the souls of Robert de Courteney, and other ancestors of the founder'. There seems little doubt, considering the Priory was dedicated not only to the Holy Trinity and St Mary but to St Thomas himself, that the foundation was piously meant as some atonement for the murder, especially as a grand-daughter of one of the other knights also left a small estate to enrich the Priory so that, as she expressed it 'the martyr might never cease to intercede for her and her children'. It is possible that the Priory had as a reliquary a chalice which had been used to catch some of St Thomas' blood on the night of the murder. Although not proven a chalice discovered during 19th century alterations at Kewstoke Church is thought to be this very reliquary, and it is now in the Castle Museum at Taunton.

A confirmation in 1262 of an earlier charter of 1230 suggests that the original foundation was at 'Dodlinch', a place never positively identified although quite possibly a Somerset house with Bristol connections, but by 1226 it had already been transferred to the present site. What is unclear is what was happening at the same time to the inhabitants of Worspring. By 1325 the canons owned all the land at Worspring that belonged to William de Courteney and Robert de Newton, but at the same time they were granted half the manor of Worle by Henry Engayne, together with the homage and dues of his tenants at Worle, Kewstoke, Milton, Ebdon, Locking and Worspring — this latter reference suggesting that some of the villagers were still living there. One may only presume that they were eventually 'phased out' by pressure from the Priory, or that possibly the ravages of the Black Death after 1349 put paid to those who remained.

The Priory itself remained small, and was not extensively endowed, the brethren being about ten in number and the revenue £87 a year. However, it was closely connected with the Weston-super-Mare Parish Church and until the Dissolution it obviously played an important part in local religious affairs. It was a uniformly well-kept house, and the only record of any trouble was in 1419, when the Prior and Canons were summoned for placing obstructions on a public path or causeway called 'Worall'. The end came with the dissolution by Henry VIII; the last Prior, Roger Tormenton, and seven canons signed the Acknowledgement of the King's Supremacy on 21 August 1534, and suppression followed in September 1536. Since that date the Priory has been used as a private residence, with a farmhouse erected between the North Aisle and the Gatehouse in 1701. In 1972, after some restoration, the Priory was opened to the public by its new owners, the Landmark Trust, and it has taken its rightful place as one of the most important historic sites in the area.

Thus Worspring ceased to be a settlement. However, all the other Domesday manors have survived, and we must now turn to the history of those which were to play significant roles in later times. Until the rise of Weston during the 19th century it was Worle which remained, as it had been in Domesday times, the most important of the local settlements. The parish church of St Martin is 12th century, although with a 15th century tower; the huge Worle Barn (of which only the buttresses survive in the Church Road Junior School), and many old cottages illustrate its long and untroubled history as an agricultural village. Probably its major claim to fame, certainly at the national level, is its place in the history of British metalliferous mining.

On Worlebury Hill, especially above Worle and Milton, can be found numerous small pits, many overgrown, which are the result of digging for calamine, the ore of zinc, and an essential requirement if England was to establish its own brass founding industry. After extensive prospecting in England for this ore, at the prompting of the government and with the help of German prospecting knowledge, it was finally discovered in 1566 on Worle Hill. A lease was taken out from its owner, Sir Henry Wallop, and miners set to work at once. An attempt to set up a brass-smelting works in part of Bristol Castle failed due to water supply problems, and it was not until 1568 that successful smelting at the Tintern Abbey works began, using Worlebury ore. There were also technical problems at Tintern however, and production, together presumably with the mining, was shortlived. Later brassmaking resumed on a permanent basis, and Worle is mentioned as being a supplier to the foundry at Isleworth, Middlesex in 1593.

Worlebury was probably the most important source for calamine in Somerset during the 16th century, although significant mining later became concentrated at Shipham and Rowberrow. All the mining was probably executed by individuals or small groups from Worle and Milton on a part-time basis, providing a useful supplement to their normal income from agriculture. This also enabled production to respond quickly to variations in demand. Rutter suggests that some working was still going on in 1829, but it cannot have survived much beyond that date.

At Uphill too a generally quiet agricultural community survived the ups and downs of English history, but the village did participate in maritime activities, and the mouth of the Axe certainly saw some trade, especially of a cross-channel nature. Arthur Salmon recorded the story of a more notorious occasion however, when in 1592 the French made a complaint to the English Government that a ship of Bayonne, returning from the Newfoundland fisheries with a valuable cargo of fish and oil was 'mett by an Englishe shippe appointed warlyke belonging to Syr Walter Rawleigh'. Raleigh's ship so 'furiously battered' the French vessel that she was constrained to yield and was brought to Uphill. This was at a time when there was not only peace but an actual alliance between the two countries. Commissioners were sent from France to sort matters out, but returned empty-handed after eight months of local delaying tactics. Bristol merchants appear to have had the profit of the cargo! There are also records of a well established trade in livestock into Uphill, and in 1666 it was recorded that at least 1160 oxen and 306 sheep were taken by sea to Uphill from Sully on the Welsh coast. In 1685 the Duke of Monmouth was urged to make for Uphill to cross to South Wales after the rebellion, and he would perhaps have taken this advice from one of his companions, Dr Oliver, had not Lord Grey checked Oliver for offering 'such foolish advice'. This story certainly illustrates the long standing trading connections of the little port on the mouth of the Axe.

Finally, Ashcombe and Weston-super-Mare through the centuries enjoyed common and relatively unchanging ownership, and, like the other local villages, a relatively uneventful history. By the 13th century, ownership of the manors had passed to the Arthur family, resident at Clapton Court near Portishead, who were descendants of the Earls of Gloucester. The earliest record of the family's local involvement is in 1229, while there is also a record of a lawsuit in 1492, when there was a dispute over the fishing rights at 'Ankers Head'. However, the family were not resident at the manors and the manor house at Ashcombe, sited off Manor Road, was really a large farm, which survived until it fell into ruin during the 19th century. Ownership passed to William Winter in 1632, this gentleman having become Lord of Clapton in 1595 by virtue of his marriage to Mary Arthur. William's grandson, Henry, was forced to sell these holdings in 1696, apparentlyto pay off the gambling debts of his father, and in that year Weston-super-Mare passed to Colonel John Pigott of Brockley, in whose family the property was to remain.

During these centuries there are few records of events in the district. It is clear that the folk of Weston were engaged in fishing, as the case of 1492 illustrates, and we must remember that in the past the Severn Estuary offered better fishing than today. Salmon were caught here well into the 19th century, and sprats were often landed in large numbers. Traditionally the fishing was undertaken using the 'stake' method, around Birnbeck island and at Anchor Head. Nets were placed between a series of stakes driven into the sea-bed at low-tide. These were then covered as the sea rose and usually the fish were caught in the submerged nets. The method had one problem however; there was a period when the tide receded during which fish were exposed but the water was still too deep to recover them. This necessitated the employment of two men, who stayed on Birnbeck Island, to act as 'gull yellers', who attempted to keep the gulls away from the catch by shouting. Some of the best yellers are said to have been audible as far away as Congresbury. In addition some fishing from boats may have occurred, although there is little written evidence of this. Farming was conducted on an open field system, early maps suggesting four large fields (West Tyning, West Field, Tor Field and East Field), these being arranged along the lower slopes of the hill, the village itself running southwards to the moor from the church in West Field along the present line of the High Street. Both the low moor and the open hill would have served as pasture.

The most prominent building in early Weston would undoubtedly have been the church. The present Parish Church of St John is the 19th century replacement, on the identical site, of the original small building, which in 1791 was described by Collinson as '84 feet in length and 20 feet in breadth, having a tower at the West end'. In the early days the Rectors of Weston were required to pay dues to the Wells Treasurer, as mentioned above, of 100 lb of wax per year. This the church seems to have had a marked reluctance to provide, for in 1277 a sentence was pronounced on the Rector for being 100 lb of wax in arrears, while action was also taken in 1309 for a 50 lb arrear. This time the 'Dean of Axbrygge' directed other local Rectors to go and collect the wax, and if this or the Rector could not be found, to sequestrate 2 marks' worth of wheat, barley and beans from his barn. While this problem continued, there were obviously other problems too, since in 1266 the Bishop of Wells actually took the living away from the incumbent because he did not attend the ordinary services.

A quieter period followed, until the Civil War, when the Rector, Christopher Sadbury, as a Royalist was in conflict with his largely Parliamentarian flock. In 1645 Sir Thomas Austen came to plunder the 'well-affected of the . . . Parish', but the parishioners, joining with friends in Milton and Worle, routed the King's soldiers. Unfortunately they later returned, and the Rector then aided their plundering. With the Parliamentary victory the villagers took legal action against the Rector, and he was found guilty, but engaged in a protracted appeal and before anything was finally resolved he was able to have the charges dropped under the Act of Pardon. Soon after the affair the Churchwarden's accounts give us a useful indication of the size of the village — for in 1694 there were 42 ratepayers, paying rates from that of £1 1s. by Edward Gorges, (at this period owner of the manor through his marriage with Grace, a daughter of William Winter), down to a minimum of 1s. The total rates collected in that year amounted to £3 8s. A total population of around 150 is possibly indicated by this number of ratepayers.

The church records also provide us with an insight into the general life of early Weston. For example, in 1353 Bishop Ralph became aware that malicious 'sons of iniquity' in the Weston area were helping themselves to the spoils from shipwrecks along the coast, despite the fact that Edward III had granted the wrecks to the

Bishop. Helping themselves to anything useful washed up on the beach no doubt continued through the centuries despite threats of excommunication. In rather later times smuggling was also said to be rife, and Weston's isolation was a great asset to this activity. Understandably however, the records of smuggling, as opposed to folk tales, are rather scant.

From the Churchwarden's Accounts, of which there is a complete set for the period 1694 to 1819, we also learn that Weston had its share of poverty, for there are numerous notes of charitable payments. 'Poore soldiers' feature as recipients on several occasions, and in 1699 1s was given 'to poore women which was undun by fire', while in 1707 a 'pore woman that was tacken by the French' received 6d. Despite its isolation Weston seems to have had its share of vagrants, and clearly the hearts of the successive churchwardens could be moved sufficiently to make some small payment, even though Weston was by no means a wealthy Parish. Even distant events moved the village, as in 1709 when 1s 6d was apparently given to aid those who suffered in the great fire in Wincanton two years earlier. On the happier side of life, there were also Weston 'church-ales', aimed at being fund-raising events for repairing the church, helping the poor or other charitable purposes. These were occasions for a general holiday and 'fun and frolic reigned supreme'. In 1699 Mr Varman the churchwarden spent 5s for a 'bushell of malt, and brewing of it', obviously providing a liberal quantity of strong ale for the parishioners. These events usually took place on a Sunday, and in 1651 it had been noted in defence of the practice, which the Puritans were then trying unsuccessfully to stop, that 'on these days the service of God was more solemnly performed, and the services better attended than on other days'.

Thus little changed over the years until the purchase of the manor by John Pigott in 1696. Although the exact dates are unknown, it appears that during the 18th century the Pigotts decided that they might use their property as a seaside retreat, and a place to which they might bring visiting friends. It is interesting to note that this was a similar pattern to the one followed by the successful Bristol-based manufacturers the Eltons, who used Clevedon Court as a summer residence in the 18th century. It seems that the Pigotts may have built a small cottage for their use, which was enlarged early in the 19th century into the substantial Grove House. The present Grove Park was developed at the same time as a private garden for this house. Meanwhile the manor farm at Ashcombe remained let to a tenant farmer, and was to play no direct part in Weston's early 19th century transformation to a seaside resort.

ABOVE: Caves at Uphill. (WM)
BELOW: Kewstoke Church.

ABOVE: Ashcombe Manor Farm in the 1820's and
BELOW: Grove House in 1829.

ABOVE: The Infirmary at BELOW: Woodspring Priory.

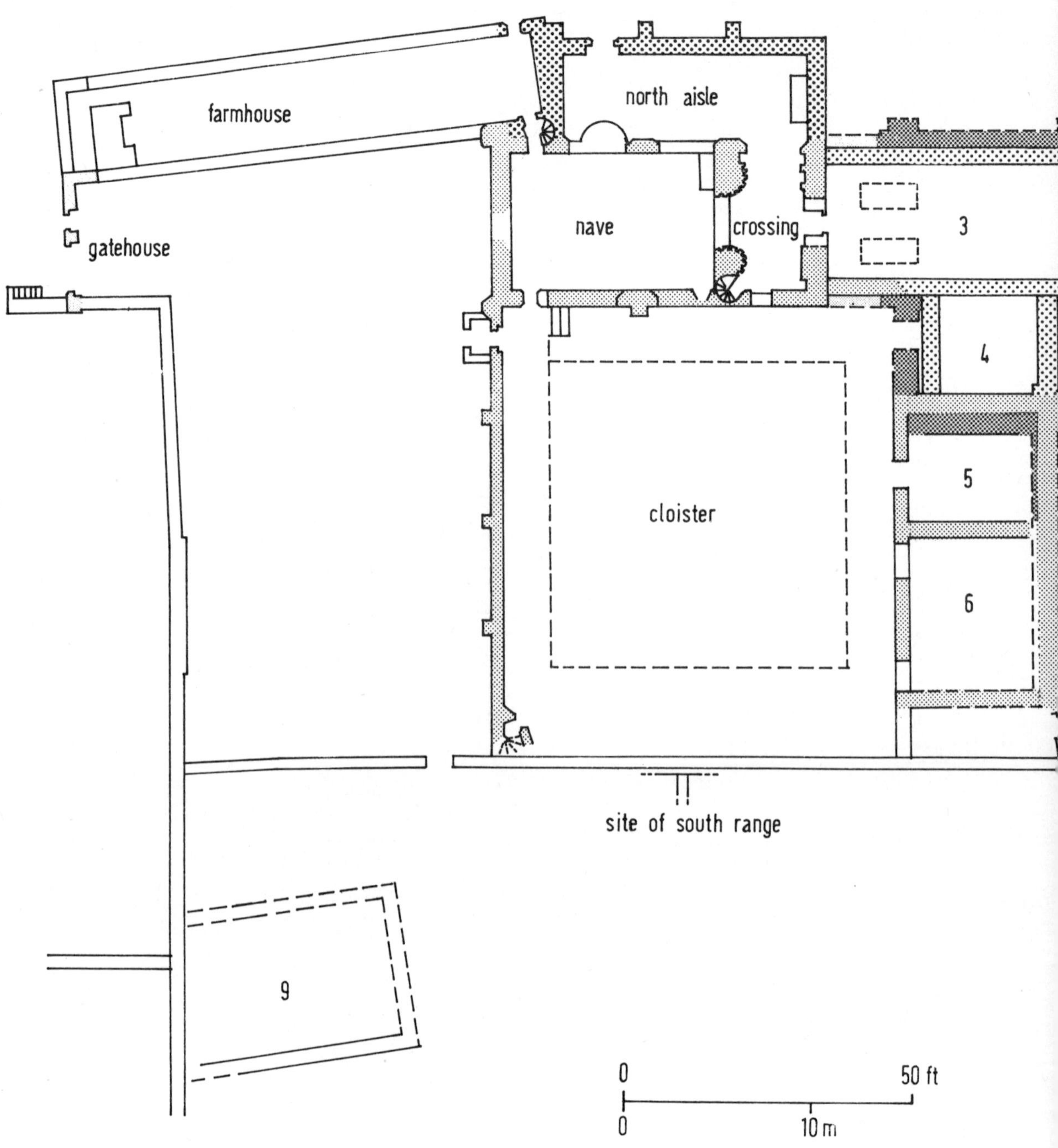
farmhouse
north aisle
gatehouse
nave
crossing
3
4
5
6
cloister
site of south range
9
0
50 ft
0
10 m

LEFT: The Priory based on a plan by kind permission of D. J. Tomalin and RIGHT: a seal from the Priory.

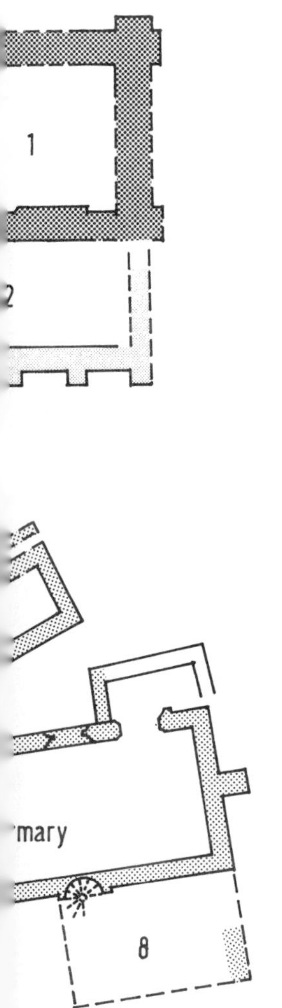

13th Century

14th Century

15th Century

15th Century destroyed

16th Century

Post - Dissolution

Excavated buildings :-

1 early chancel
2 lady chapel
3 later chancel
4 sacristy
5 chapter house
6 parlour ?
7 reredorter
8 infirmary chapel
9 undated building

N.B. conjectural walls shown with broken outline.

ABOVE: Uphill Church, 1829 and BELOW: St. Martin's Church, Worle with INSET: detail from a window in the first Parish Church replaced in 1824. (WM)

SOMERSETSHIRE.

Worle Inclosure.

The Commiſſioners appointed for carrying the Act of Parliament for this Incloſure into Execution,

Do hereby give Notice,

THAT THEY SHALL PROCEED TO SELL,

(IN FEE)

By Public Auction,

At the VALIANT SOLDIER Inn, in the Pariſh of WORLE,

IN THE SAID COUNTY OF SOMERSET,

On FRIDAY the 22d Day of JANUARY, 1802,

Between the Hours of FOUR and SIX o'Clock in the Afternoon,

THE UNDERMENTIONED

LANDS;

Subject to such Conditions as shall be then & there produced.

LOT I.

A Piece or Parcel of Paſture Land, called Worle Hill, containing by Admeaſurement 112 Acres, 3 Roods and 24 Perches; well known to be an excellent Sheep Sleight, and to be ſupplied with Spring Water in the drieſt Seaſon.

LOT II.

A Piece or Parcel of Land, containing by Admeaſurement 11 Perches; being an Encroachment made from Worle Hill aforeſaid, and uſed as a Garden by —— Biſhop, bounded Eaſt Weſt and North by Worle Hill, and Southward by Garden Ground adjoining the ſaid —— Biſhop's Cottage.

LOT III.

A Piece or Parcel of Land, Part of a Piece of Ground called the Bowling Green; containing by Admeaſurement 15 Perches, and bounded on the Eaſt by Lot 4.

LOT IV.

A Piece or Parcel of Land, alſo Part of the ſaid Bowling Green; containing by Admeaſurement 14 Perches; adjoining Lot 3 on the Weſt, and Lot 5 on the Eaſt.

LOT V.

A Piece or Parcel of Land, alſo Part of the ſaid Bowling Green; containing by Admeaſurement 5 Perches; adjoining Lot 4 on the Weſt.

LOT VI.

A Piece or Parcel of Land, called Dock Hill; containing by Admeaſurement 22 Perches; bounded Eaſt and Weſt by Roads, and North by a Garden belonging to Mr. Dennis Sheppard Leman.

LOT VII.

A Piece or Parcel of Land, containing by Admeaſurement 1 Rood and 15 Perches; bounded Eaſt by old incloſed Lands belonging to Mr. George Yeo, and Weſt by a Road called Moor Lane.

☞ For viewing the Premiſes apply to Mr. JOHN BISHOP, of Worle aforeſaid; and for further Particulars of Sale to Mr. JAMES STAPLES, Land-Surveyor, No. 12, Bridge-Street, Briſtol; or to SAMUEL BAKER, Attorney at Law, Blagdon, Somerſet.

S. BONNER, PRINTER, CASTLE-GREEN, BRISTOL.

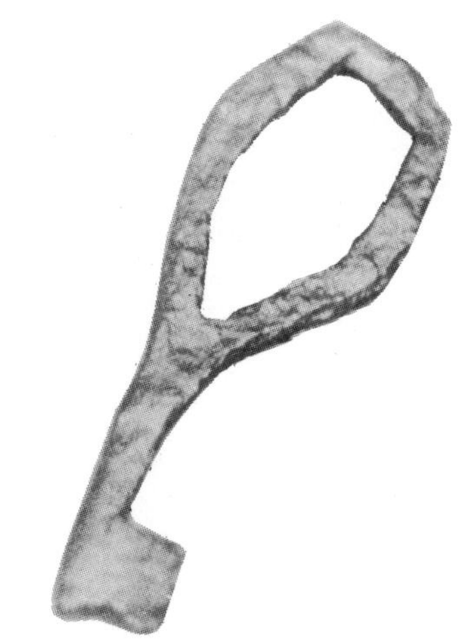

LEFT: Sale of land at Kings Head, Worle. RIGHT ABOVE: Worle Windmill, c. 1871 and BELOW: a key, probably 12th century, found in Worle. (WM)

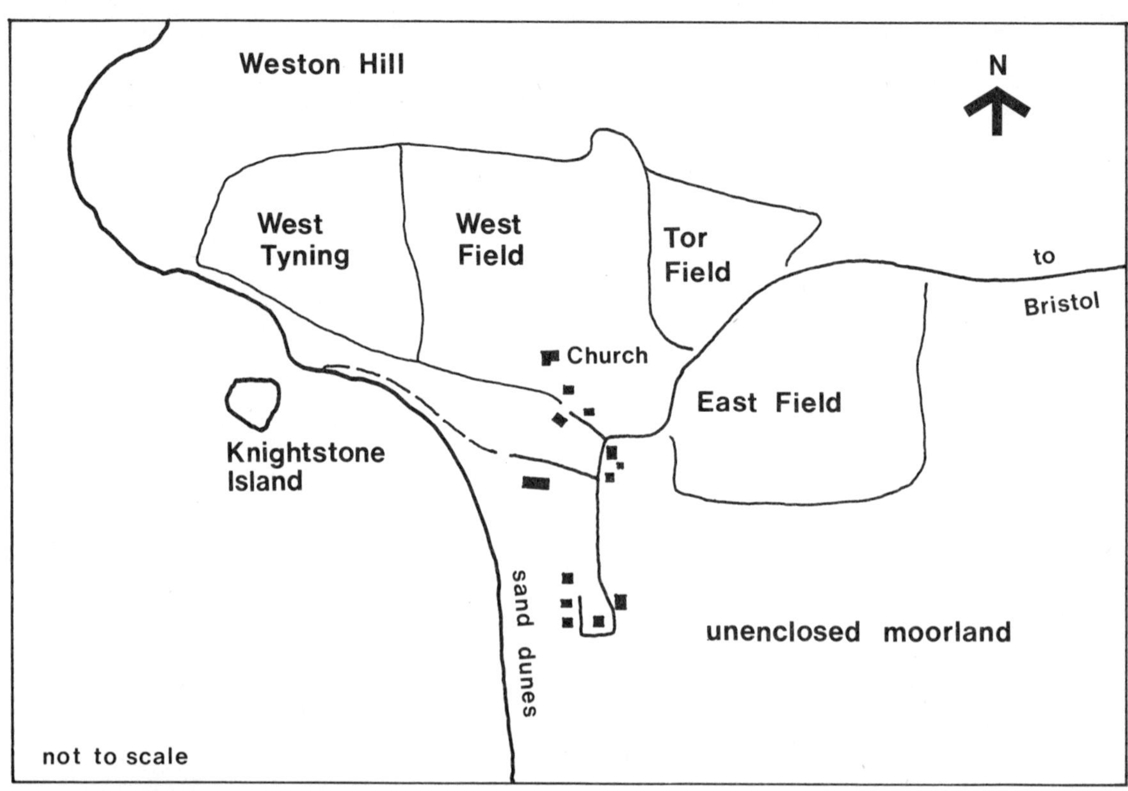

ABOVE: The village and open fields of Weston before enclosure, and BELOW: Worle in the 1900's.

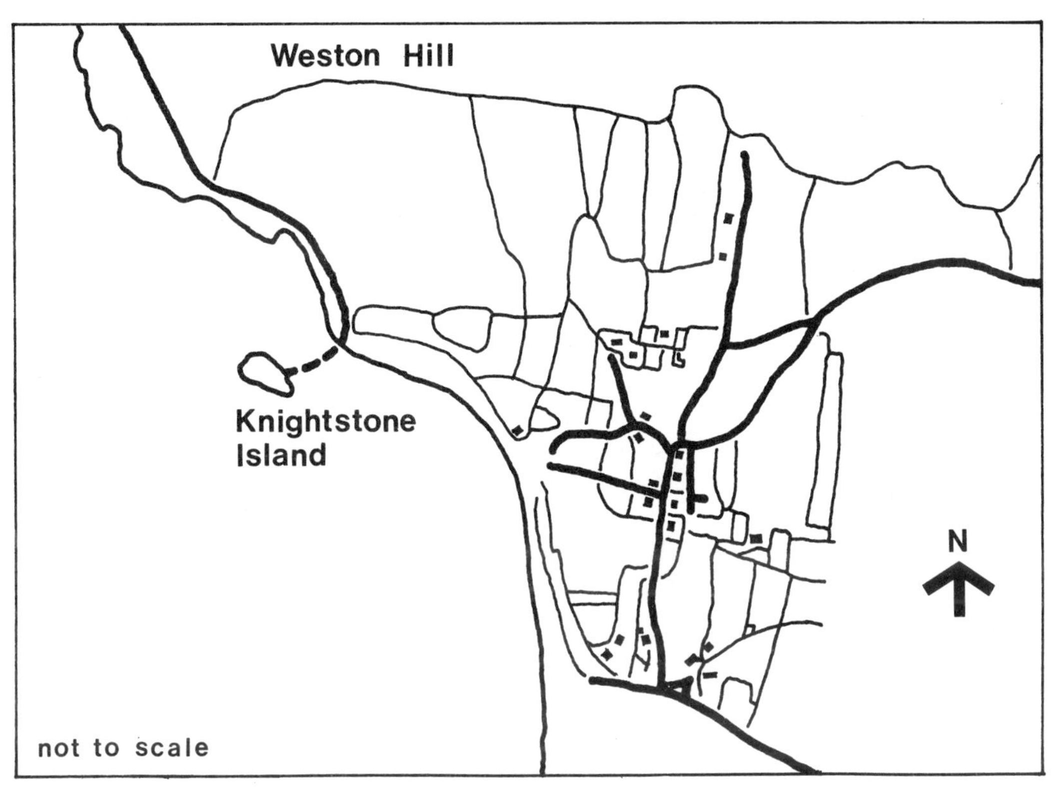

ABOVE: Weston-super-Mare in 1806 and BELOW: Weston Bay in 1829.

The faces of Weston — LEFT: Rev Wadham Pigott (1750-1823) Rector of Weston, (WM), CENTRE: John Hugh Smyth Pigott (1792-1853), Lord of the Manor, and RIGHT: a corbel from the original parish church. BELOW: The old church, demolished in 1924.

The Foundation

It is now hard to imagine what Weston was like before its development as a seaside resort, yet that is what we must do if we are to understand the tremendous changes which occurred in the early 19th century. Weston had changed little through the centuries up to 1800, when a few small cottages and rough shanty dwellings of fishermen were to be found strung out along the single street, sheltering behind the sand dunes which fringed the whole bay. Above the church and village rose the barren grassy slopes of the hill, whose appearance would have been rather like that of Middle Hope or Brean Down today. The hill was largely unfenced, and like the ill-drained moorland which then stretched between Weston and Uphill, was held in common for the grazing of sheep and cattle. The village street, now High Street, was just a track, too narrow to allow carts to pass each other. It was not paved, and was said to have been muddy and dirty, although as a concession some stones were thrown down on one side to make a sort of footpath.

Even in an age when the great cult of sea-bathing was taking hold among the aristocracy and gentry, and when the best medical opinion was endorsing both sea bathing and the drinking of sea water for the cure of an assortment of ills, in all fairness Weston-super-Mare in 1800 did not offer itself as an ideal place for a major resort to rival the likes of Brighton, Margate or Weymouth. Although its scenery may have pleased the more romantically minded, all the environmental drawbacks of large estuaries were present, including muddy water and a high tidal range which with the gently sloping foreshore caused the sea to retreat almost out of sight at low tide. These were not attributes which an aspiring publicity officer would wish to mention in the town guide in order to attract holiday visitors. In Weston's case such basic problems were compounded by its physical isolation in the ill-drained marshlands, and the story of the foundation of the resort and its successful growth is therefore all the more interesting as a real triumph over adversity.

The first hint of change came when the Pigott family began using their Weston property as a summer residence, and during the later 18th century there were other occasional visitors to Weston Bay mainly seeking recovery to health. The most notable of these was Hannah More, the renowned worker for social and educational improvement among the poor in Somerset. She visited Uphill in 1773 and during her stay formed an acquaintance with Dr Langhorne of Blagdon, who was staying in Weston itself. Then in 1791 the Rev William Leeves, Vicar of Wrington, built a small cottage at Weston as a summer retreat, a portion of his formerly picturesque building surviving today as part of the Thatched Cottage Restaurant. Another short visit was described by the Banwell antiquarian George Bennett in the 1805 edition of *Gentleman's Magazine,* but this showed that visitors were not then expected in Weston! However, Bennett's writings did bring Weston to the notice of a wider public, although his description of the view from Worlebury Hill as 'wild, grand, awful and terrific' might be thought a little too eloquent.

By this time there had already been some recognition of the potential, which was illustrated by the following advertisement from the *Bonner & Middleton's Bristol Journal* of 29 April 1797:

'For Health and Sea Bathing. At Uphill in Somersetshire. Jane Biss and Son most respectfully inform the public that they have fitted up two commodious Houses for the reception of Families or Single Persons during the summer, on reasonable terms, where it will be their study to render every accommodation in their power. The situation at Uphill is universally allowed to be healthy and pleasant. Pleasure boats and Passage Vessels to the Holmes or Welsh Coast. Uphill is 13 miles from Bristol to the Churchill Turnpike on the Western Road;from Churchill to Uphill 8 miles.'

Despite repeated advertisement no development at Uphill followed, and we must conclude that Jane Biss and son were unsuccessful in their enterprise. Their attempt did however show that around Weston Bay the potential of such activity was seen, and that it could be developed given the right circumstances. These came about in the village of Weston between 1800 and 1820.

The first and most important fact was that in 1803 a Yorkshireman named Richard Parsley moved to Weston to become the major tenant farmer of the manor and resident steward of the Pigott lands. Although little is known of his early life his actions show an energetic and resourceful man who must be regarded as the founder of resort Weston. Probably prompted by his arrival and ideas the Pigotts began to revise the distribution of landholdings, and during 1807 sold many of the smaller holdings to Parsley and John Cox, who was another Pigott tenant from Brockley. The details of these events are unrecorded, but it is said that some of the inhabitants, apparently fishermen who had been squatting in various dilapidated cottages and huts, were evicted, although some had lived there for many years in amicable relationship to the manor estate.

Parsley and Cox were mainly concerned with acquiring the common rights attached to these 'Auster Tenements' (small cottages with historic rights of common), for although both continued to farm profitably, Parsley for example growing teazles for the Yorkshire woollen industry, they had already decided that Weston might be developed as a resort. One key to development was the creation of a new pattern of land ownership, dividing up the 993 acres of common land that then existed. Thus Parsley and Cox were the prime movers in attempts to obtain an Act of

Inclosure, although they were supported by the Pigotts, who had extensive knowledge of the agricultural benefits which such action brought for large landowners. To apply for an Act the consent of two-thirds of the landowners was needed, which was why ownership was so important for Parsley and Cox. Weston was actually one of the later parishes in the area to be enclosed, being preceded for example by Yatton in 1751, Bleadon in 1788, and Worle in 1801.

The Weston-super-Mare Inclosure Act was passed by Parliament in 1810. As was normal an Enclosure Commissioner, James Staples, was appointed to organise the process, which consisted of dividing up the available land in a rational way among those with rights of common. The costs were high, and had to cover the making of new roads and tracks, planting hedges, digging ditches, building walls and stabilising dunes. They were met by selling some of the land at auction, and this was clearly intended for use as building land, as it was on the present sea front between Regent Street and Severn Road. At an auction in 1811 James P. Capell, the tenant of the farm at Ashcombe, bought 25 acres of this land for £38 an acre, while Mr Isaac Jacobs, a wealthy Bristol glass manufacturer, bought a smaller plot on which he built 'Belvedere', Weston's first holiday villa, on the site of what is now the Beach Bus Station. Mr Colston bought the land on which Richmond Street was eventually built and Mr Stevens that on which Carlton Street developed.

The enclosure process was completed quite rapidly, and the final *Award,* giving details of all the changes and improvements, was made in 1815. The resultant ownership pattern was one of some fragmentation, especially along the sea and dune frontage, and was most suitable for the speculative development which Parsley and Cox were encouraging. The Award Map, which is the earliest depicting Weston with any accuracy, is clearly a blueprint for the future growth of the town, and during the 19th century the pattern of development was closely governed by its provisions.

While the enclosure was taking place, Parsley and Cox began work on another part of what we may now see as their 'Master Plan' to develop Weston, the building of an hotel, which as well as providing accommodation might act as a spur to other speculative building. In partnership with J. P. Capell and a Mr Fry they financed the construction of an hotel on the site of an old farmhouse which had been destroyed by fire in the late 18th century. Considerably altered and expanded this building is now the Royal Hotel. There is doubt about the date when the hotel first opened, but contemporary newspaper reports indicate that construction began in 1808. It was certainly completed in 1810, when it was leased to James Needham, a Bristol hotelier. It opened in July of that year supported by a sequence of advertisements in the Bristol newspapers:

'Sea Bathing. Weston-super-Mare, Somerset. 20 miles from Bristol — 30 ditto from Bath. James Needham, respectfully informs the Public he has fitted up the HOTEL with every convenience, for the accommodation of large and small parties and families; and hopes by assiduous attention in every department, to obtain the honor of their patronage.

A select Boarding Table — Neat Post Chaises — Good Stabling and lock-up Coach Houses.
For bathing and the Salubrity of the Air Weston has received the decisive sanction of the first Medical Characters in Bath and Bristol.
J. N. begs to notice, the delay in opening the House, having arisen from unavoidable circumstances; he trusts a generous public will excuse any disappointment they may have hereby experienced.'

The first hotel was an important landmark in the foundation of any new resort, but was always rather a gamble for the investors. Weston's was no exception, and the doors closed through lack of custom in 1811. They remained so for three years, but between 1811 and 1814 the number of visitors to the village seems to have risen gradually. Weston began to acquire a reputation among the doctors of Bristol and Bath, and more generally among the wealthy public, as a health resort within convenient reach of their homes, and it must have been quite an adventure coming to the little village and staying in what would have been rustic and primitive conditions in the existing farms and cottages. The visitors had little to entertain them except the sands and the sea; even beer was infrequently available, a bell being rung in the streets to announce its sale in the hotel. Nevertheless visitors came, and not only did the hotel re-open in 1814 but in that year the first passenger coach service from Bristol probably began. The first sign that the resort had arrived on the social scene was the publication in 1815 of an *Arrivals List* in the *Bristol Mercury*. From then on its place as a resort for health and pleasure was established, and during the 1820s it received much favourable comment in the West of England's newspapers. All this had been achieved, unlike many of its counterparts elsewhere, without any royal or aristocratic associations, Weston depending for its support on the lesser gentry and the growing numbers of the professional and middle classes.

Thus by building the hotel, encouraging publicity and investment, and organising the land ownership to their advantage, Parsley, Cox and others had begun a complex process of development. Their own actions should be seen in a wider context however, for everything was to no avail if Weston could not be reached easily, and if goods and services were not available for visitors within the village. Fortunately the early 19th century brought a great improvement in road communications to Weston. There were two routes from Bristol at that time, the first along the present line of the A38 reaching Weston via Churchill, Banwell and Worle, the second, and more convenient, through Long Ashton and Congresbury. The latter route was greatly improved by the late 18th century turnpiking of the road as far as Congresbury, while the 1809 Congresbury, Wick St Lawrence and Puxton Inclosure Act created a passable road across the moor to Worle. Flooding of the Congresbury to Worle section was, however, only finally cured by the 1819 Congresbury Drainage Act which straightened the course of the River Yeo. Both routes were in use by coach services until 1828, when the Banwell one was abandoned, regular summer coaching from Bristol having commenced in 1818.

From information in contemporary coaching directories it seems possible that the coaches could have brought as many as 5,000 staying visitors during the summer season of 1820, and perhaps 7,000 by 1840, considerable numbers for a small resort at that time.

The route taken by the majority of these coaches through Long Ashton and Congresbury was an easy one containing few difficult gradients, but the final approach to Weston was not, the only road into the resort from Worle being on the hillside from the Scaurs and Church Road in Worle to Bristol Road in Weston. This route was a legacy of the days when the moorland was undrained, and involved several steep gradients 'rendering the use of the drag-chain brake necessary three times in as many miles'. Nothing was done to improve the situation for many years presumably because the traffic was not that heavy. Eventually a Turnpike Trust was formed to join the existing Parish roads of Weston and Worle, since the Highways Board consistently refused to act. The short Weston-super-Mare and Worle Turnpike, running from the western end of Worle High Street to the present junction of Locking Road and Baytree Road, opened in 1840, and tolls were collected until 1882. No trace now remains of the Turnpike Cottage and gate.

The improved roads also enabled the establishment of a regular carrier service. The earliest recorded carrier was the four-times-a-week cart from Worle to Bristol run by Messrs Stabbins and Wallis in 1806, but this was soon discontinued. It was not until 1811 that a regular carrier was operating, this time to Weston itself. This first Weston carrier was James Harse (1787-1874), and he was typical of the people who grasped the opportunities offered by tourism and made their living from providing the basic service functions of the early resort. Harse was a native of the small village of Badgworth near Axbridge, but had been employed since about 1800 by James Capell on the Ashcombe Manor Farm. In 1811, having realised the potential for a carrier to the new resort he bought a wagon and began what proved to be a successful enterprise. By 1818 he had diversified and was responsible for most of the post-chaise hiring in the area, and was also renting a large portion of the Pigott estate in Weston as a farm. In the carrier trade he was not without competition however, for two others began operating in 1813 (Roger Harris and James Pearce), and by 1820 there were eight. These services helped to place Weston in touch with the outside world, and brought in for the first time in any quantity externally manufactured goods. Visitors could then be provided with all the comforts of home. Almost everyone in the village of Weston joined with the carriers in providing both services and accommodation for the visitors, finding that on the whole this could be a profitable activity, and thus together with the 'founding fathers' Parsley and Cox, the inhabitants themselves were also the creators of modern Weston.

The first guidebook for Weston was published by John Chilcott of Bristol in 1822. It was able to note the rapid rise of the resort, which was 'now a fashionable summer retreat, and by the last census taken in May 1821 consisting of seven hundred and thirty-five souls'. 'The purity of the air, added to its vicinity to Bath and Bristol, attracted the attention of valetudinarians; and the cures continually effected by the uncommon salubrity of its invigorating breezes, soon raised it to the station it now occupies amongst fashionable watering places'. The guide is an interesting document offering comment on the village and many surrounding places, and suggesting many activities and walks for the visitor; however its most important paragraph relates to Weston itself:

'Weston-super-Mare does not present a very inviting appearance to the stranger. The houses, scattered mostly without arrangement, and roofed with red tile, give a character of meanness to the village: and if a stranger first enters it on a stormy day and at low water, he may perhaps feel inclined to turn his horses' heads towards home again; however, a walk to Claremont Lodge and over the hill, would even then convince him that Weston has at all times attractions; and his surprise at the metamorphosis will be great if he patiently awaits the flowing tide. On a fine summer evening nothing can be more beautiful than the scene which it presents; numerous groups walking on its extensive sands, a variety of carriages of all descriptions, horses, ponys, donkeys, wheel chairs, &c., fishermen shrimping, and the villagers enjoying the high tide after the labours of the day.'

An alternative view of Weston-super-Mare in 1819 comes from the following extract from a letter written by Mrs Thale Piozzi, a friend of Dr Johnson:

'This little place is neither gay nor fashionable, yet full as an egg insipid as the white on't, and dear as an Egg o'Penny. I enquired for books, there was but two in the town was the reply, a Bible and a *Paradise Lost*'.

Even by 1822 Weston was clearly able to offer a considerable variety of accommodation, the result of speculative building undertaken mainly by various local inhabitants. In addition to the original hotel, by then known as Fry's Hotel, there was also the Plough Hotel, (built in 1819, now demolished), several terraces of houses which could be rented for the summer, various villas and cottages and, at a distance from the old village, Claremont House, built in 1816, which is mentioned in the 1822 guide as 'a beautifully situated lodging house'. The house was demolished in 1866 to make way for Claremont Crescent. By 1829 it was claimed that there were 150 lodging houses in the resort, and although perhaps an exaggeration it is likely that nearly all the buildings were being used to take paying guests or were let as furnished accommodation. Lodgings could be obtained from about 2 guineas per week to as much as 6 guineas, at a time when in contrast the average wage of an agricultural labourer in Somerset was only seven or eight shillings per week plus 3 or 4 pints of cider a day! Small wonder then that the villagers were willing to aid the growth of the tourist trade.

In these years before the coming of the railway, visitors were mainly of two types, both drawn largely from the middle and professional classes of Bristol and Bath. Predominating were family groups: mother, children and sundry relations renting furnished rooms or a whole house for themselves and a few servants. They stayed for most of the summer season, joined for shorter periods by the head of the household when his work or obligations permitted. In smaller numbers came the individuals in search of recovery to health, their servants, and the occasional physician. These parties, together with a slowly increasing number of leisured residents, provided the basis for developing shops, libraries, bathing establishments and other trades, and also led to the beginning of community action to improve the public amenities.

The small island of Knightstone was purchased in 1820 by a Mr Howe from Bristol, and it was he who erected the first medicinal baths there, which were rented in 1822 by Benjamin Atwell. At that time the island was connected to the mainland by a ridge of pebbles, but since this was covered at high tide visitors often had to be rowed to and from the island. The Rev T. Pruen bought the island in 1824, and he made several improvements, including constructing a low causeway which was above high tide level, and building an open air swimming bath on the shore of the island facing Glentworth. Further development on the island was carried out by Dr E. L. Fox (the noted pioneer of the humane treatment of the insane at his private hospital in Brislington) and his son Dr F. K. Fox, so that with its baths and lodging houses Knightstone was an important feature of Weston's health resort facilities during the 1830s. At about the same time as the development of Knightstone Mrs Gill's baths were opened in Somerset Place. These were less elaborate, and 'the water was hauled from the sea in a barrel and stored in a tank over a boiler in which it was heated, and, by means of pipes running through a wall, supplied the baths. She also had a shower bath, a good old-fashioned "Punch and Judy Box" affair in which the victim stood . . . whilst a bucketful of sea water was poured over his head from the top by an assistant standing on steps'.

Sea bathing for health and pleasure in the muddy waters of the Bay was also commonplace by the 1820s. Anchor Head was one of the most popular bathing places — indeed it may have been the original bathing site — and it is interesting that there were only three bathing machines on the sands in 1822, economy perhaps triumphing over propriety. Changing for bathing on the beach without a machine remained common, and Weston's machines never acquired the 'modesty hoods' common at Margate and Weymouth, which shielded bathers from view as they descended into the water. Later in the century some controls on bathing were made by local by-laws, but on the whole these were not too strictly applied. The Weston bathing machine, simply a changing room on wheels, was of a simple design, with wheels of equal size since the beach was almost level. Most of the machines were built and operated by Joseph Burge, who was the sole local manufacturer until 1855, although some were also operated by the Harvey family from the 1840s.

Apart from its natural attractions early Weston offered few amusements. The 1822 Guide could suggest the use of the billiard table 'near the hotel', or the reading room in Knightstone, commanding a fine marine view, where the newspapers were taken daily. There were two pleasure boats for hire, kept by 'careful and experienced fishermen', and the amusement provision was completed by the availability for hire of 'Jaunting Cars, wheel and sedan chairs, ponies and donkeys'. A small library and reading room was opened by Richard Hill at 2, South Parade during 1824, supplementing the otherwise meagre facilities.

The 1820s saw many other changes. In order to accommodate the greater numbers of visitors the old Parish Church was pulled down in 1824, being replaced by the present building which opened in 1825. Two private schools had opened: May's Boarding School in Weston and Brickmans Academy (which was in Worle but advertised the advantages and salubrity of the situation near Weston). Then in June 1825 the first pleasure steamer called at the Knightstone Wharf bringing passengers from Newport, and such was the increase in visitor numbers generally that the first attempt by the community to improve the resort was decided upon. This was the construction of the first section of the esplanade, between the Knightstone Causeway and Leeves Cottage, in 1826, followed by its extension to Regent Street in 1829. Richard Parsley, John Cox and especially John Reeve, who was by then the proprietor of the Hotel, were the main instigators of this work, which was partly paid for by public subscription. The esplanade, on the site of former sand dunes which had been levelled during enclosure, was a gravelled path fronted by a low wall, hardly elaborate, but providing the first public promenade off the beach. Further facilities added in the 1820s included John Thorn's Assembly Rooms, (now part of the Beach Hotel), which date from 1826, and the first Market House, built by Richard Parsley on the site of the present Playhouse Theatre. Finally, at this time John Hugh Smyth-Pigott began the planting of Weston Woods, the actual work being carried out by James Atkins. After initial problems in getting the trees to grow on the thin limestone soils and exposed slopes the planting was successful, so that by the middle of the 19th century the whole appearance of the hill had changed, the woods contributing greatly to the Weston scene.

The Weston 'season' was at first limited to the summer, and William Norvill commented that 'none of the people would bide here in the winter, they always said it would be too cold, they couldn't stand it', but the 1830s saw some winter visitors in search of a good convalescing climate. One of the few surviving accounts of such a visit is that by William Prieaux, young son of a prominent woollen draper and silk merchant in Bristol. William began his convalescence at Clevedon, but did not like it there and moved with his servant to Weston in late December 1839. In a letter written to his father in Bristol he commented 'we had a little walk up to Knightstone baths on Saturday, which was a tolerably fine day; and yesterday was still more so, we had such a nice scramble over Anchor Head rocks, and it was nearly high tide so that it was very pleasant'. In another letter he remarked on a visit to Knightstone Baths saying 'I have had four baths and liked them pretty well'. William returned home in March, apparently much recovered.

In February 1889 the *Weston Mercury* reported an evening lecture by Rev H. G. Tomkins on the theme 'Memories of Old Weston'. Mr Tomkins said he remembered first coming to the resort in 1834, having been brought here by his family after an attack of 'juvenile whooping cough', from the effects of which the recuperative air of Weston, combined with donkey rides on the 'health-producing sands', speedily restored him. He remembered having lodged in Carlton Street. It was the first time he had ever seen the sea, and he recollected the astonishment of his Berkshire nurse on seeing the bathing machines on the sands and her wondering 'what they kept such large dog kennels for'! He noted that the hill had recently been planted, but one could see over the tops of the trees and enjoy the prospect.

There are few other surviving contemporary comments by or about the visitors to village Weston. One however stands alone in its intuitive interpretation of the resort, a poem published in the *Bristol Mirror* in 1824 called 'Lines on Leaving Weston':

Farewell to thee Weston! I loved thee before!
And each visit I pay thee endears thee yet more;—
So healing, so bracing, so pure is thy air,
Can any inhale, and its virtues not share?
So varied thy walks, so extensive thy beach,
Old and young, sick and healthful, thou'rt suited to each.

Farewell to thee Weston! — as yet Child of Nature;
May Art never mar thy original feature;
Nor thou, in *vain* efforts to rival gay places,
Forget thy best charms are anomalous graces;
Whilst tyrannical Fashion elsewhere cramps our ease,
Be thy motto — "At Weston ALL do as they please".

During the pre-railway era Weston seemed to offer a charm that was the very reverse to that of fashionable Brighton, having essentially rural and romantic attraction. Perhaps this was a reflection of the heritage brought to it by the majority of its Bristolian visitors, who were content to enjoy it without severe social order, were traditionally divorced from the fashion-conscious influences of London, and some of whom were close to the romantic movement in English literature. Thus in terms of its social development as well as a consideration of the place of origin of its visitors, Weston-super-Mare was a truly West Country resort. Its development before 1841 had been impressive and it was well placed to attract far greater numbers of visitors as the railway age began.

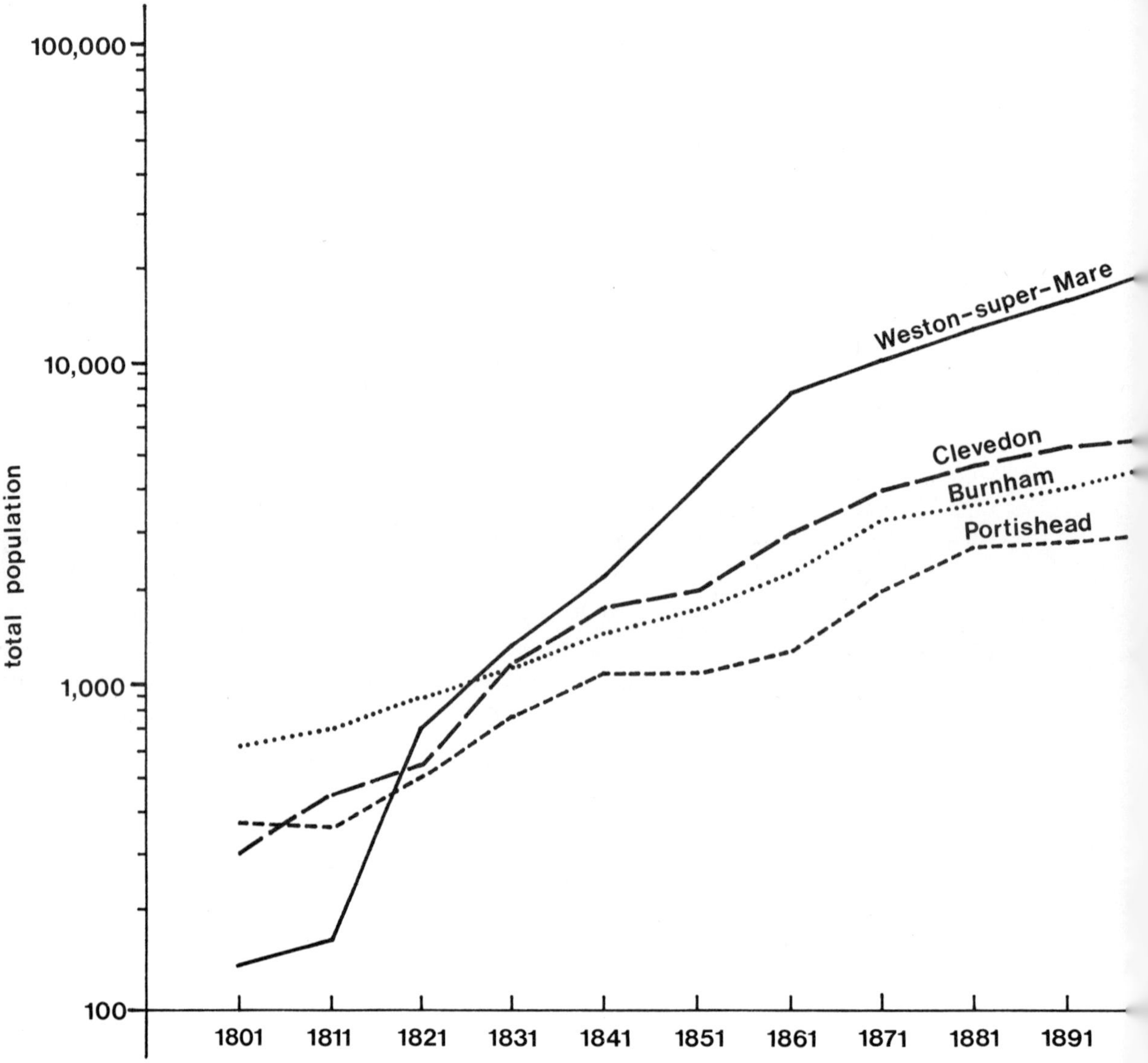

100,000

10,000

1,000

100

total population

Weston-super-Mare

Clevedon

Burnham

Portishead

1801 1811 1821 1831 1841 1851 1861 1871 1881 1891

ABOVE LEFT: Rectory and Glebe, Waterloo House and Worlebury, 1815, (WM), RIGHT: Weston in 1801, BELOW LEFT: the growth of population compared to rival Somerset resorts and RIGHT: cottages and boat sheds in 1815. (WM)

ABOVE: View to sea, Verandah House on the left and Hotel on the right, 1815. (WM) CENTRE: Leeves Cottage, Parish Church and the Hotel (now Royal) that year (WM) and BELOW: the 1815 High Street. (WM)

ABOVE: Leeves Cottage in 1820 and BELOW: Billy Board's Cottage at Claremont.

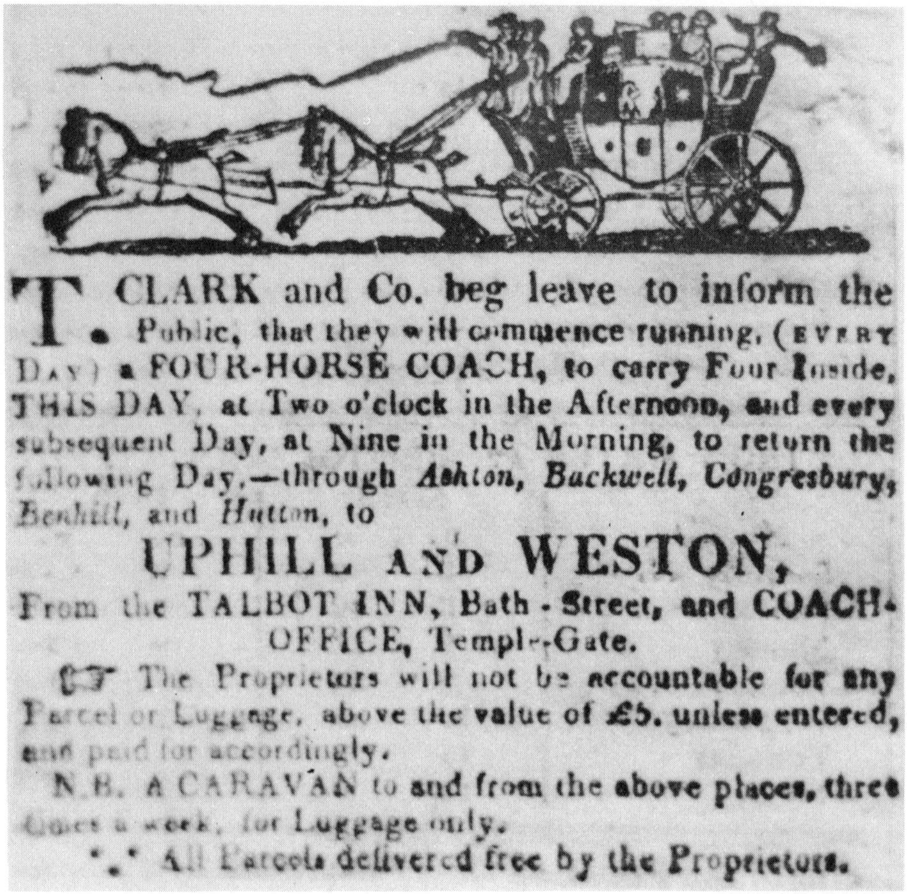

T. CLARK and Co. beg leave to inform the Public, that they will commence running, (EVERY DAY) a FOUR-HORSE COACH, to carry Four Inside, THIS DAY, at Two o'clock in the Afternoon, and every subsequent Day, at Nine in the Morning, to return the following Day,—through *Ashton, Buckwell, Congresbury, Benhill,* and *Hutton*, to

UPHILL AND WESTON,

From the TALBOT INN, Bath-Street, and COACH-OFFICE, Temple-Gate.

☞ The Proprietors will not be accountable for any Parcel or Luggage, above the value of £5, unless entered, and paid for accordingly.

N.B. A CARAVAN to and from the above places, three times a week, for Luggage only.

⁂ All Parcels delivered free by the Proprietors.

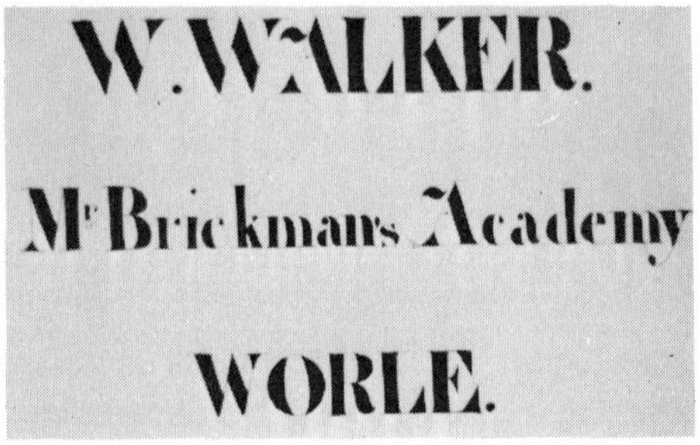

W. WALKER.

Mr Brickmans Academy

WORLE.

ABOVE: Carrier's advertisement, Bath — Weston-super-Mare, 1816, BELOW LEFT: handwriting exercise from Brickman's Academy, Worle and RIGHT: Dr Fox of Brislington, owner of the first Knightstone Baths.

TEN GUINEAS REWARD

For Apprehending and Taking the Body of

JAMES HILL, of MILTON,

In the Pariſh of *Kewſtoke*, in the County of *Somerſet*,

On Suſpicion of the WILFUL MURDER of

BETTY LIGHT, of the ſame Pariſh,

A Child about SIX Years and Half old, by committing a RAPE on her Body.

HE is about five Feet ten Inches high, 28 Years of Age, ſerved in the Somerſet Militia from the Year 1787 to 1792, has dark ſandy ſtraight Hair, weak grey Eyes, pale Complexion, long Noſe with a Blemiſh on one Side of it, is thin grown, has a long Chin and Neck, is Knock-knee'd and walks with his Toes turned pretty much outward.

The above Reward will be paid on Delivery of the aforeſaid JAMES HILL to WM. SHEPPARD, Church-Warden, or SAMUEL DAY, Overſeer of the aforeſaid Pariſh.

Dated the 2d of May, 1794.

PRINTED BY S. BONNER, CASTLE-GREEN, BRISTOL.

Poster offering reward for the capture of a murderer in 1846.

ABOVE: Knightstone Causeway and Island in 1837, CENTRE: bathing machines and BELOW: Weston from Worlebury in 1853.

ABOVE: Weston from Worlebury in the 1840's and BELOW: Knightstone and the beach early in that decade.

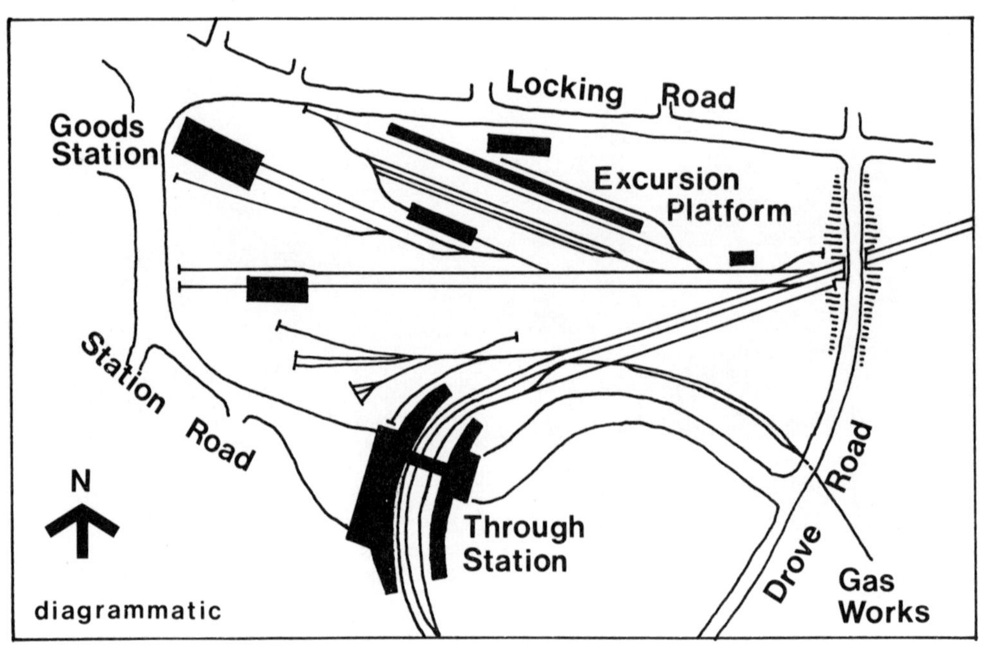

ABOVE: Swiss Villa — used as a base by Brunel during the building of the Bristol and Exeter Railway and BELOW: Weston's railway stations in 1900.

Coming of the Railway

There can be little doubt that the coming of the railway was the most important event in Weston's history. In the railway mania of the 1830s it was inevitable that Bristol should be connected to London at an early date, and this broad gauge line was completed in 1841 by the Great Western Company under the direction of the famed Isambard Kingdom Brunel. It was only logical that the iron way should also extend south-westwards to Exeter, and thus while the GWR were driving their tracks to Paddington the separate Bristol and Exeter Company, who also employed Brunel as engineer and used the broad gauge system, built their lines across the Somerset lowlands. The Bristol and Exeter Railway Act of 1836 took the main line in a sweeping curve which was at its nearest point about one and a quarter miles from the centre of Weston. The pressure of opinion and difficulties over the acquisition of land had led Brunel to avoid the resort, many of the landowners being against the noisy and smoky railway, thus only by means of a second Parliamentary Act in 1838 was Weston to be provided with its own short branch line and station. This sort of situation was not unusual, and was adopted at several locations by Brunel, but Weston had missed a golden opportunity of being on the main line, and for over forty years passengers had the inconvenience of changing trains in the middle of nowhere just for the brief ride to the town.

For a time during the construction of the line through Somerset, Brunel and his family lived at Swiss Villa, a large picturesque house off Locking Road, which although now demolished is remembered in the name of Swiss Road. They were not to remain long however, for with few physical barriers to overcome the line was completed rapidly. Indeed, it has the distinction of being one of the few main lines ever built which came within its estimated cost! Despite its missed opportunity Weston nevertheless became one of the first seaside resorts in the world to receive a rail link, and services began on 14 June 1841. The original branch line left the present main tracks at Weston Junction on Hutton Moor, where a small platform, primitive waiting room and ticket office had been provided, and followed a straight course along the line of what is now Winterstoke Road to the original station. This was situated on Alexandra Parade, adjoining the present Anchor Hotel and overlooked by the Victoria. The Anchor was formerly known as the Railway Hotel, and was another of Richard Parsley's many investments in the town. The station was thus on the edge of the then built-up area of the town, but conveniently close to the sea front for excursion visitors.

For the first ten years of operation, passengers for Weston were carried, rather slowly if the journey was against the wind (when it could take up to half an hour), in small, light open-sided horse-drawn carriages. Each train consisted of 3 four wheeled coaches drawn by 3 horses in tandem fashion, and it was said that some passengers preferred to walk, since it was frequently quicker! In 1851 the horses were replaced by a small steam locomotive, and in its turn the small terminus station was replaced by a new and larger one, beyond the Locking Road, in July 1866, on a site behind the present Odeon cinema, thus obviating the busy level crossing on that route. This new building was, however, soon destined to become the goods station, for in response to the heavy traffic and growth of the town the GWR, which had absorbed the Bristol and Exeter in 1876, decided to abandon the branch and build a loop line and through station. This, the present passenger station, was opened after some delay in 1884, providing a much improved rail service and giving Weston direct main line connections to London, the Midlands and South Wales. Previously, in 1875, the Bristol and Exeter tracks had been converted to the standard gauge, and on 18 July of that year the first direct excursion trains arrived from Birmingham, opening up a large new market for the resort. The part of the old branch line linking the gas works on Drove Road was retained until production ceased in 1968. Land adjacent to the old terminal station, which itself became the goods depot, was then developed as the excursion station, to service the many special trains run at the main holidays, and with this Weston's conventional railway facilities reached their zenith.

Although at first the horse-drawn branch line trains placed limitations on traffic, the railway was from the beginning a great success, and its opening brought about the almost instant withdrawal of the stage coach services from Bristol. Many more people began arriving as travel was so much easier, and the impact on the town was immediate. Indeed, this impact had been anticipated, and although the number of visitors had been rising slowly in the late 1830s (after a stagnation during the early part of that decade), it was the impending arrival of the railway which had pushed up the price of land such that when numbers one and two South Parade were for sale in 1837 the newspapers noted that 'as building land cannot be obtained but at a very great price, such an opportunity as the present [sale] may not present itself again'. Joseph Whereat, founder and editor of the *Weston Gazette* was able to note with satisfaction in 1845 that 'our town is fast enlarging and improving, the past few years have made many alterations to the number and neatness of its shops. We think there is every reason to believe that the fears entertained by the many that the Bristol and Exeter Railway would carry the usual visitors of Weston into Devonshire are likely to prove quite groundless. Weston-super-Mare is found to be just at the most convenient distance from Bristol and Bath, in that gentlemen can easily bring their families hither, and come and return by early and late trains without interruption of their normal hours of business'.

In fact it was estimated that in 1844 some 23,000 visitors arrived by rail, an increase of the order of 300% on the figures for the end of the coaching era only five years previously. It is also significant that this figure would have included few day visitors, and the economic impact of such a large number of resident holidaymakers must have been immense.

The first cheap day excursions from Bristol to Weston probably ran during 1846, although the first written account of such an outing is from 1847, when some 1,200 employees of the Stothert Iron Works arrived. They were closely followed by a party of 2,000 from the Great Western Cotton Works, whose excursion was to become an annual event. All the early excursions were organised by individual groups of workers from single industries who had hired their own trains, and it was not until Whit Monday 1851, after the horse-drawn carriages from the Junction had been replaced by steam, that the Bristol and Exeter introduced their own public excursions. On the first of these from Bristol some 2,000 people arrived to take the Weston air, and for many it must have been their first visit to any seaside. They obviously liked what they saw, for the excursions were a great success and set the pattern for the rest of the railway era. In the following year the first excursion from Bath ran, although this only attracted 600 passengers. Neither were the local residents denied the advantage of cheap rail travel, and as early as 1853 an excursion to Exeter and back, accompanied by a brass band, was organised by Mr Phillips. The fare was the princely sum of 4 shillings. Then in 1855 there was an excursion to London, offering three days in the capital for only 7s 6d (or 12s 6d first class). By the late 1850s the railway company had really become organised in the excursion business, and by 1857 were even running evening trips from Bristol to Weston on a regular basis throughout the summer.

The railway came to Weston at a time when the increasing prosperity of the Victorian age was enabling the growing middle classes to copy their social superiors and take a holiday by the sea. The basis of Weston's growth and prosperity was this solid middle class support, combined with an increasing number of permanent but leisured residents who had the financial means to vacate the unhealthy industrial cities to which so many of them actually owed their prosperity. Normally these people had the resort to themselves, and were able to promenade, bathe or saunter along sands and hill without difficulty. Problems arose however when at the popular public holidays the large crowds of excursionists arrived. They brought little financial benefit to Weston, many spending nothing in the town as they had brought picnics with them, but crowded the promenade and streets, although they mostly appear to have enjoyed themselves immensely.

At first all was well, and the *Weston Gazette* noted in June 1848 that the behaviour of the Great Western Cotton Factory excursionists 'was generally very creditable', but as numbers increased so sometimes did behaviour problems. Thus in 1856 the *Gazette* commented:

'We have during the past week been visited by thousands of excursionists from

Bristol. The fare was very low (7d and 1s 2d) and brought the dregs of St Philips, Bedminster and other disreputable neighbourhoods. They destroyed every quiet retreat. It was of course out of the question for our two constables to deal with 5-6,000 persons. If these conditions continue the future of Weston-super-Mare as a fashionable resort is at stake. What invalid would dare to emerge from lodgings on such a day?'

Obviously there were occasional fights, (Weston's cabmen were often a target as crowds waited impatiently for their excursion trains home), and perhaps too much drinking in the pubs, but it all amounted to little; most people came simply to enjoy a day by the sea and enjoy it they did. Thus although the numbers continued to rise, from 5,000 in the 1850s to 15,000 on Bank Holidays in the 1870s and 20,000 in the 1890s, there was little crowd trouble, although there was plenty of overcrowding.

Neither were there any serious problems on the railway itself, even though as early as 1855 the branch line was 'proving inadequate to carry all the passengers'. There was only one serious railway accident on the branch which occurred on 2 April 1865, when at the Junction a down express ran into the branch line train, which had been delayed on the line by a breakdown. Several people were seriously injured, and the shed which served as a waiting room was demolished. It appears that there was no telegraph connecting the Junction with Puxton Station, and thus no means of warning the express to stop. Another accident, less dramatic, occurred in 1847, when one of the horses pulling an evening train from Weston to the junction fell dead from heart failure right across the track. The carriages were derailed, and the passengers walked the remaining mile to the Junction.

As the 19th century progressed Weston also saw many more visitors coming by the Bristol Channel steamers, especially from the Welsh ports, and also many more local day visitors coming by road on everything from farm carts to early bicycles. Yet the railway remained the main form of transport until the Second World War, although its supremacy was challenged by cars throughout the present century. Even in 1901 it was noted that 'motor cars were in evidence to an unprecedented extent', and by 1937 nearly as many people came by car as by train. Today about four out of every five visitors come by car. The total number of visitors to the town has also risen rapidly. Bank Holiday excursion records have been continually broken, August holiday crowds totalling 51,000 in 1921, and 78,000 in 1937, while more recently estimates of 100,000 excursionists have not been uncommon. Thus during the 1970s Weston has been receiving annually some 350,000 staying holiday visitors and 3 million excursionists, and together they bring nearly £20 million annually to the local economy. But it was the railway which inspired and aided this growth, and which produced the essence of Victorian Weston, and we must not forget that it also brought more than a little seaside pleasure to millions of working families in Britain's 19th century industrial towns, for whom Weston was an ideal seaside playground.

£100

FOR

TWO PENCE.

EXCURSIONISTS

MAY SECURE A PROVISION OF

ONE HUNDRED POUNDS FOR THEIR FAMILIES

IN CASE OF DEATH

BY

RAILWAY ACCIDENT,

With an allowance of £1. 0s. 0d. per Week for themselves if laid up by Injury,

BY TAKING AN

INSURANCE TICKET

COSTING

TWO PENCE.

☞ ASK FOR AN INSURANCE TICKET WHEN YOU PAY YOUR RAILWAY FARE.

Railway insurance in the 1860's.

Leeves Cottage in 1883.

ABOVE: the first railway station 1841-1866 and BELOW: Weston-super-Mare station in 1896.

LEFT: Edwardian beach scenes; CENTRE: soldiers leaving during World War I and excursionists arriving in the '20s; RIGHT: the beach in 1937 and a commemorative jug. (WM)

ABOVE: Rozel — Dutch Oven and BELOW: the floral clock in 1936.

ABOVE: The famous Weston donkeys on the beach and BELOW: Professor Staddon's Punch and Judy, 1932.

ABOVE: Marine Lake in 1951 and BELOW: in the 1960's.

Victorian Town

After an initial burst of development between 1815 and 1830, by which time the resident population had risen to 1,300, Weston entered a quiet period when there was little building or change. This seems to have been due largely to the rapid rise of Clevedon in the early 1830s, which not only captured the attention of the regional press but also many potential visitors to Weston. This situation did not last long, Clevedon's popularity waning, and almost coincident with the accession of the young Queen Victoria in 1837 Weston entered a new phase of expansion, this time with the confidence and expansive spirit of the Victorian age.

Until this time areas of new building had been limited, largely confined to the core of the old village and on the land near the beach and dunes sold at enclosure. The only fully built-up districts were the working class areas between Regent Street and Carlton Street and the northern part of the High Street. From 1837, with the building of the main railway line begun, many development possibilities were seen, and much land was made available for building, including the Glebe Land between the Church and the sea, and parts of the Smyth-Pigott estate. Such was the speed and extent of the building that by 1855 *Woods Excursionists' Guide* could comment that 'seven or eight years ago the Beach, Park Place, Victoria and Albert Buildings, may be said to have comprised the chief ranges of private dwellings and lodging houses. Since that period an immense impulse has been given to building enterprise. As if by magic there have sprung up Oriel Terrace, the Crescent, Greenfield Place, Prince's Buildings, Manilla Crescent and Wellington Terrace fronting the hill; together with an almost equal number of streets and houses, of less note, in different parts of the town.'

Building continued with more and sometimes less rapidity throughout Victoria's reign, paralleled by rapid increases in Weston's population: from 1,113 at the 1831 census to 1,469 by 1841, 8,038 in 1861 (a doubling in one decade), and more steadily to 23,235 in 1911.

The Victorian town which resulted from this expansion, largely built with local grey limestone, did not grow without planning and structure. Although the restrictions of modern legislation did not apply, much care and consideration was exercised by the many individual developers, and good judgement by the landowners, ensuring that Weston remained attractive to both residents and visitors. The essential Victorian Weston, rather neglected in our own century, has much of interest, and is undoubtedly worthy of careful conservation.

Although it is impossible to detail here the growth of the town building by building, it is possible to identify four main lines of development of the Victorian town. The first of these consisted of a number of large prestigious buildings which were of a much grander conception than any of Weston's earlier developments and aped those of the larger spas. These consisted of terraces and crescents and began with the terraces along Knightstone Road. Victoria Buildings date from 1840, and these were followed by Albert and Prince's Buildings, linking the Knightstone Causeway with the village. These and other projected developments were the reason for the application for an Act of Improvement in 1842. This brought effective local government to Weston for the first time, with the election of an 18-strong Board of Improvement Commissioners. They had powers to levy rates and borrow money, and were responsible for lighting, paving and draining the town. It is significant that most of the original members, such as Francis Hutchinson Synge, the chairman, Richard Parsley and his son Horatio, William Cox, John Palmer and Dr F. K. Fox, had played or were to play important parts in the development of the resort. They stood to benefit from the success of the town, and were obviously motivated to provide by public action the basic facilities necessary for civilized holidaymaking and residence.

The solicitor Henry Davis (1807-1868), who had set up a practice in Weston during 1837, was appointed to the influential position of Clerk to the Commissioners. 'Lawyer' Davis was to become one of Weston's most successful building speculators, and it was he who obtained the lease on former Glebe land and built first Oriel Terrace and then Royal Crescent, both dating from 1847. These developments were on a much larger scale than previous building, and their success led to further speculation producing Wellington Terrace in 1849, Manilla Crescent in 1851 and the later Claremont Crescent in 1865. It also inspired Ellenborough Crescent (1855), the first of many buildings on the Whitecross Estate. This had been Richard Parsley's farm, and was a creation of the 1810 enclosure. It was bought for development after Parsley's death by Henry Davis and Joseph Whereat, the latter being the proprietor of the *Weston Gazette,* and was later acquired by the British Land Company.

The houses in these fine crescents and terraces were both let for the holiday season and used as permanent homes, but more favoured for residence during the second half of the century were the large villas, detached and semi-detached, set in their own gardens. This was the second type of development in 19th century Weston, and it has created perhaps the largest single element in Weston's Victorian townscape. Villas were built as estate developments but more often by individuals, but the landowners controlled the general pattern of building. Nevertheless there was scope for a great number of variations on the basic theme.

By the end of the century large areas of the favoured hillside areas and the low ground south of the centre had been covered with buildings. It was said that some 40 villas were under construction as early as 1844, but most date from after 1850. The Shrubbery Estate dates from the 1850s, building at Montpelier had begun in 1858, South Road developed in the 1860s, and the Eastfield Park Estate in the 1870s, while villas at Trewartha Park date from 1898. In the lower part of Weston the Whitecross estate saw building from 1858 onwards, Clarence Park estate from 1888 and the Newcombe estate from 1901. Although many of the villas could be rented on short or long term bases, they were essentially the residences of a leisured class which included retired service officers, industrialists, clerics, writers and professional men — people who formed the backbone of Weston society.

Much of the hillside land had been owned by the Smyth-Pigott family and the development of their estate is the key to Weston's later 19th century growth. The estate, which was administered for much of this crucial period by Robert Landemann Jones (commemorated by the name of Landemann Circus), gradually released land as market conditions dictated. The normal procedure was to lease land (or sell it subject to a perpetual rent charge), but to impose upon it strictures relating to the time limits for the commencement of building, the price of the houses, building lines and street patterns, thus regulating development to the aesthetic advantage of the town without incurring any direct charge upon itself. By influencing the availability of land the estate indirectly affected many sectors of the town economy, for example by varying the employment prospects for workers in the various building trades and at the Royal Potteries, and by aiding the increase of accommodation for visitors and residents. The first recorded leases were in 1846 on sites in Wadham Street, followed in 1849 by sites in Victoria Crescent and Wellington Terrace. Sales of land reached peaks in the late 1850s (South Road and Church Road), the early 1870s (George Street, Bristol Road), and the late 1890s and early 1900s (Hatfield Road, Hughenden Road, Milton Road). For the modern town the most significant development by the Smyth-Pigott estate was the creation of the Waterloo Street and Boulevard link to the Montpellier Estate. The roads were made after 1860, and the villas lining the Boulevard mostly date from the 1880s. The Boulevard was deliberately planned in the Parisian style, with the view of Christ Church spire as its focus.

Three of the roads dating from these periods, South Road, George Street and Hatfield Road, are worth consideration in greater detail, for they illustrate how the development of the estate's land changed during the century. The land on the northern side of South Road was leased within the decade 1858-1867, and most of the large detached houses which still occupy the site were completed during that period. Samuel Harvey, Alfred Hawker and Samuel Morgan each built two properties, while Edward Locock originally took leases on three sites but was only able to complete building on two (his option on the third being taken by John Palmer in 1864). All of the remaining plots were, however, leased and developed by individuals, who had villas built for their own use. Great George Street (now

George Street) was disposed of between 1871 and 1875, and largely built during those years. In contrast to the mansions of South Road, George Street was intended as a middle class development, with semi-detached villas of an unpretentious character suitable for use as guest and lodging houses. William Willcox leased 11 out of the 67 plots and was the largest single developer, but nearly the whole road was built as a series of small speculations. Finally, in Hatfield Road, leased between 1898 and 1901, nearly all the building was by E. E. Baker and A. F. Milkins.

Between 1862 and 1872 it was estimated that the estate had increased its rent roll in Weston by an average of £2,500 per annum, had built 250 houses, given land to the town for use as roads valued at £25,000, and spent a similar amount on roads themselves. In total some £250,000 had been contributed to the local economy during the decade in what was the period of most intense development of the estate. A similar if smaller scale pattern was followed by the other estates, of which the Whitecross was the largest, resulting by 1900 in two distinct arms of villadom stretching both east and south from Knightstone. These extensive residential areas of the middle classes were largely Anglican in persuasion, and to serve them the original Parish was sub-divided during the century and new churches built. Emmanuel was the first to be established, in 1847, followed by Christ Church in 1855 and Holy Trinity in 1862. All Saints and St Saviour's followed, with St Pauls in 1912 reflecting the rapid growth of housing beyond the Sanatorium at that time. In contrast the non-conformists were originally to be found among working and professional people of the town itself, and the chapels were thus located near the town centre — the Wesleyan of 1846 at the corner of St James Street being replaced by a larger one in 1860 (now Barclay's Bank) and the Congregational in High Street, which is now a part of Messrs Woolworth's store. Later in the century a spread of the non-conformist interest is reflected by Bristol Road Baptist Church, which dates from 1871.

During this period Weston also acquired further working class residential areas, which are the third type of development. By the 1840s the first such area, between Regent Street and Carlton Street, had been virtually fully built up, with terraces of smaller houses, shops, workshops and even the small gasworks. Consequently a new working class community developed on the land with lower amenity value (having neither good views nor easy access to the promenade), between the Boulevard and Locking Road. Building here began with terraces in Orchard Street and Meadow Street during the 1850s, Palmer and Hopkins Streets during the 1860s, and the Clarendon Road area (built for artisans by the National Freehold Land Society) later in the same decade. Meadow Street became the main shopping focus for this community, which included the boatmen, blacksmiths, plasterers, painters and all the other trades needed by the town. In addition the houses were also used as holiday accommodation, the often large Victorian families somehow making room for the welcome paying guests in the season. These areas were substantially built, and are still largely intact, forming an interesting and historically valuable pa Victorian Weston.

Finally, but by no means of least importance, the fourth area of development after 1850 was the town centre. Although some of the earliest resort development had taken place around the north-eastern part of the High Street, in 1841 much of what is now Weston's principal shopping street remained undeveloped, the main growth of retailing having been in St James' Street. However, linking as it did the two main 'growth areas', and running close to the promenade, the potential of High Street was seen during the 1840s, when most of its eastern side was filled with buildings, many of which were shops. By the later 1850s the High Street had become the main shopping street, having 42 out of the total of 84 shops then open in central Weston.

As well as shops, offices and many public houses, the town centre also began to acquire a range of public buildings. On the site of the present Playhouse Theatre the first Weston market building opened in 1827, to be replaced in 1858 and again in 1900. The town's second assembly rooms (now replaced by new shops) opened in 1858 at the corner of West Street and High Street. A Congregational Chapel was built in 1830, to be replaced by a larger one in 1855 which is now incorporated in Messrs Woolworth's premises, and the first phase of the present Town Hall dates from 1859. The Town Hall was considerably expanded in 1897 to the design of Hans Price, while the clock tower was added in 1927. Price was Weston's most prolific 19th century architect, designing several of the main public buildings including the School of Science and Art, now part of the Technical College. He was also responsible for many of Weston's houses both grand and humble, and undertook commissions in Clevedon, including the castellated Pier Toll House. Of the many other buildings of note are Emmanuel Church, the Albert Memorial Hall of 1862, and the Library Building in the Boulevard from 1900. Thus by 1900 the town centre was fully built-up, and with a variety of shopping streets, a long covered arcade and numerous substantial public buildings, fully able to provide for the needs of residents and visitors alike.

As the town expanded so did the problems created by urban living, and for a resort like Weston two problems faced by all 19th century towns were of particular importance — the provision of a good water supply and the safe disposal of sewage. Until the Improvement Act of 1842 these were the responsibility of the individual householder, with water being drawn from numerous wells and sewage often being discharged directly into the many small rhynes now lost under asphalt and concrete. The possible pollution of drinking water by sewage therefore became a major question as the town grew, for the prosperity of the resort could have been severely damaged by even rumours of health dangers, much of the publicity for Weston emphasising its status as a health resort. The newly-elected Board of Improvement Commissioners were not slow to realise this, and one of their first actions was to obtain a report on the sewage problem from the Market Committee late in 1842. Directed by Mr Armstrong, a civil engineer who was also employed by Bristol

Corporation, work began on a sewage system early in 1843 and was complete by the November of that year. Armstrong had apparently considered the possibility of placing the outfall at Anchor Head, but objections on grounds of cost and beach pollution forced the deposition of raw sewage into a rhyne draining through Uphill into the River Axe.

This proved to be an unsatisfactory arrangement, and led in 1850 to a legal dispute with Uphill over pollution there. The matter was only resolved by the construction of depositing tanks for partial treatment of the sewage in 1852. The tanks were leased as a source of manure at a nominal rent to the Chairman of the Commissioners, F. H. Synge. Even this solution soon came in for criticism, for with the town still growing rapidly there were many complaints about the drains and potential pollution. The *Gazette* commented in 1854 that 'should it become known that the drainage is defective, it will no longer become the resort of the health-seeking invalid.' For many years however, the Commissioners adopted only minor palliatives, until once again legal proceedings were threatened over the state of Uphill Great Rhyne in 1865. Forced into action the Commissioners then took the bold step of employing the eminent Victorian engineer Sir Joseph Bazalgette (who had developed the drainage system for London) to design a completely new system. Although an interesting rival scheme to reclaim 1,000 acres of Sand Bay by pumping Weston's sewage there was suggested by J. H. Smyth-Pigott and Mr Hellier, it was the Bazalgette scheme which was adopted, and completed by the contractor Mr Gaskell by the end of 1866. This scheme, the cornerstone of which was a new main sewer from Orchard Street direct to the mouth of the Axe, served the needs of the growing town for the next century, during which period there were few drainage problems.

Improved drainage had eased the danger from well water, but problems still remained for the lower part of the town. Thus in 1852 the leading inhabitants, led by Henry Davis, took action themselves by forming a Water Company, which later received the support of the Commissioners. Although it had been intended originally to bring a supply from the Mill Pond at Banwell, trial bores at Ashcombe early in 1854 produced an abundance of water and public supplies from the reservoir at Montpellier began later that year. In 1865 a new reservoir was constructed on Worlebury to supply the higher parts of the town, and the company operated profitably until its purchase by the Commissioners in 1878. At this time the Commissioners also obtained powers to supply Uphill, Worle and Kewstoke, although it was not until the end of the century that supplies were made available in these villages.

However, even in the 1870s it was noted in a Government report on river pollution that Weston's drinking water was of sometimes questionable quality, particularly that which was still obtained from wells near the town centre, and it was only at the end of the century that a mains supply was fully accepted in some households. Fortunately for Weston the potential health dangers were never realised, and the town remained one of the healthiest of watering places, escaping throughout the century the worst ravages of disease. In the Registrar General's Quarterly Report of August 1871 figures were given for the death rates in 47 resort towns, whose population by then totalled over 1 million. The national annual average was 18 deaths per 1,000 population, the lowest was Folkestone with 11 per 1,000 and Weston was close to this with 12 per 1,000 — highest was Aberystwyth with 25 per 1,000. Victorian Weston was thus not only well built, sensibly planned and visually attractive but a clean and healthy town in which to live and play.

View from Spring Hill in 1865 — from a painting by Sheppard. (WM)

LEFT: Baytree Road 1865 by Sheppard, (WM) RIGHT: Parsley's Tower, commemorating the 1832 Reform Bill by a pigsty capped by a bishop's mitre, (WM) and BELOW: High Street in 1900.

ABOVE: The first Atlantic cable comes ashore in 1885, CENTRE: Whereat's Reading Rooms, Regent Street 1842, and BELOW: Park Place.

LEFT: 'Dad' Comer, Town Crier till he was 88; ABOVE RIGHT: Montpelier Lodge, 1870; CENTRE: Villa Rosa, 1848; BELOW: Royal Hotel, 1864. INSET: F. Hutchinson Synge, first Chairman of the Town Commissioners, 1842-1854.

ABOVE: Congregational Church, High Street in the 1850's, now Woolworth's; LEFT: Christ Church and RIGHT: Emmanuel — at the same period. INSET: Boulevard Congregational Church, destroyed in 1942.

LEFT: Knightstone Harbour in 1858, RIGHT: Knightstone Causeway five years earlier, and BELOW: Weston seen from Knightstone.

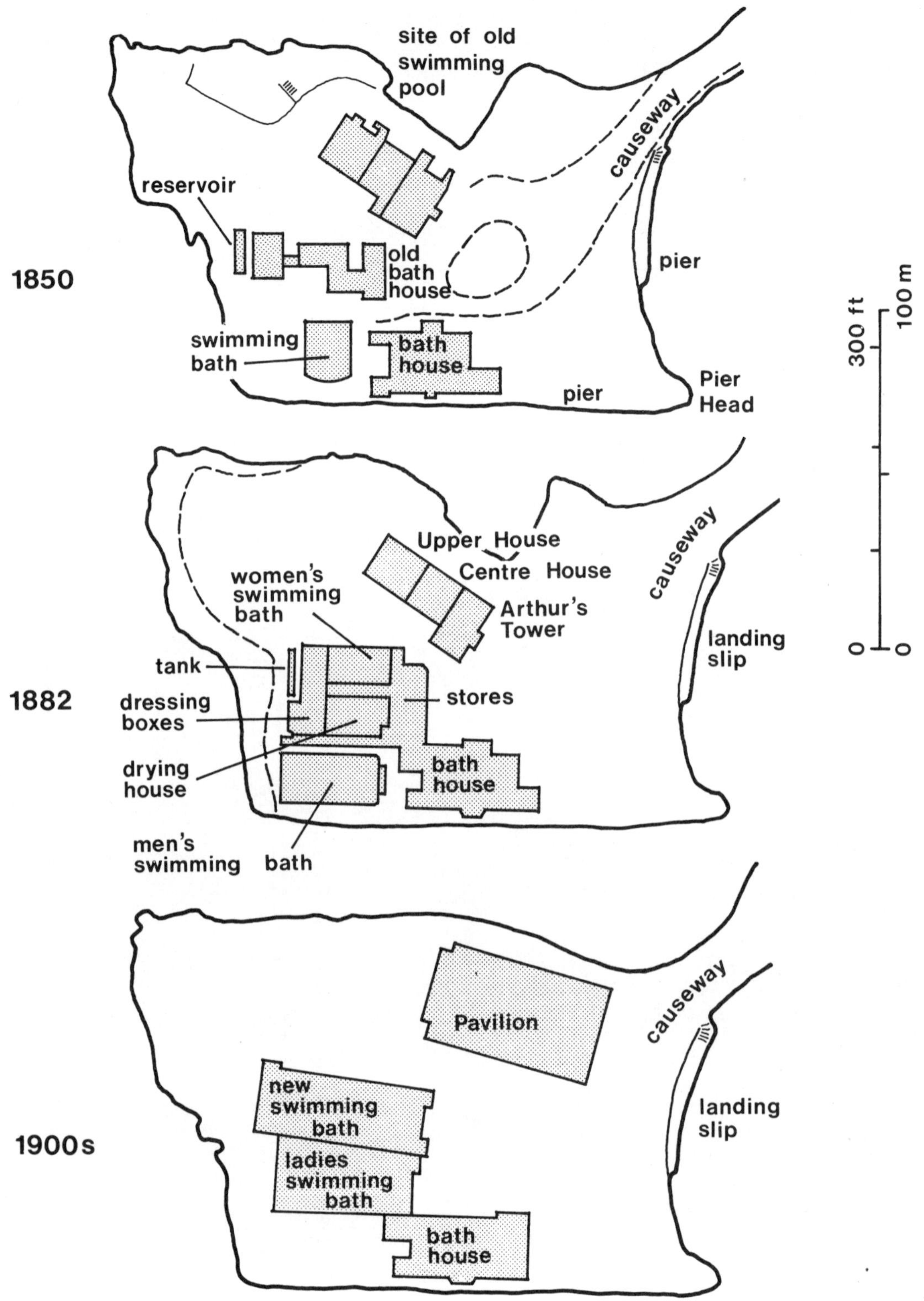

Knightstone's development from 1850-1900.

ABOVE: Ellenborough Crescent in 1864; CENTRE: Town Hall and Emmanuel in 1861 and BELOW: Oriel Terrace.

ABOVE: Atlantic Terrace in 1876 and BELOW: Weston promenade and beach around 1867.

ABOVE: The Police c 1870 and BELOW: the Fire Brigade in 1888.

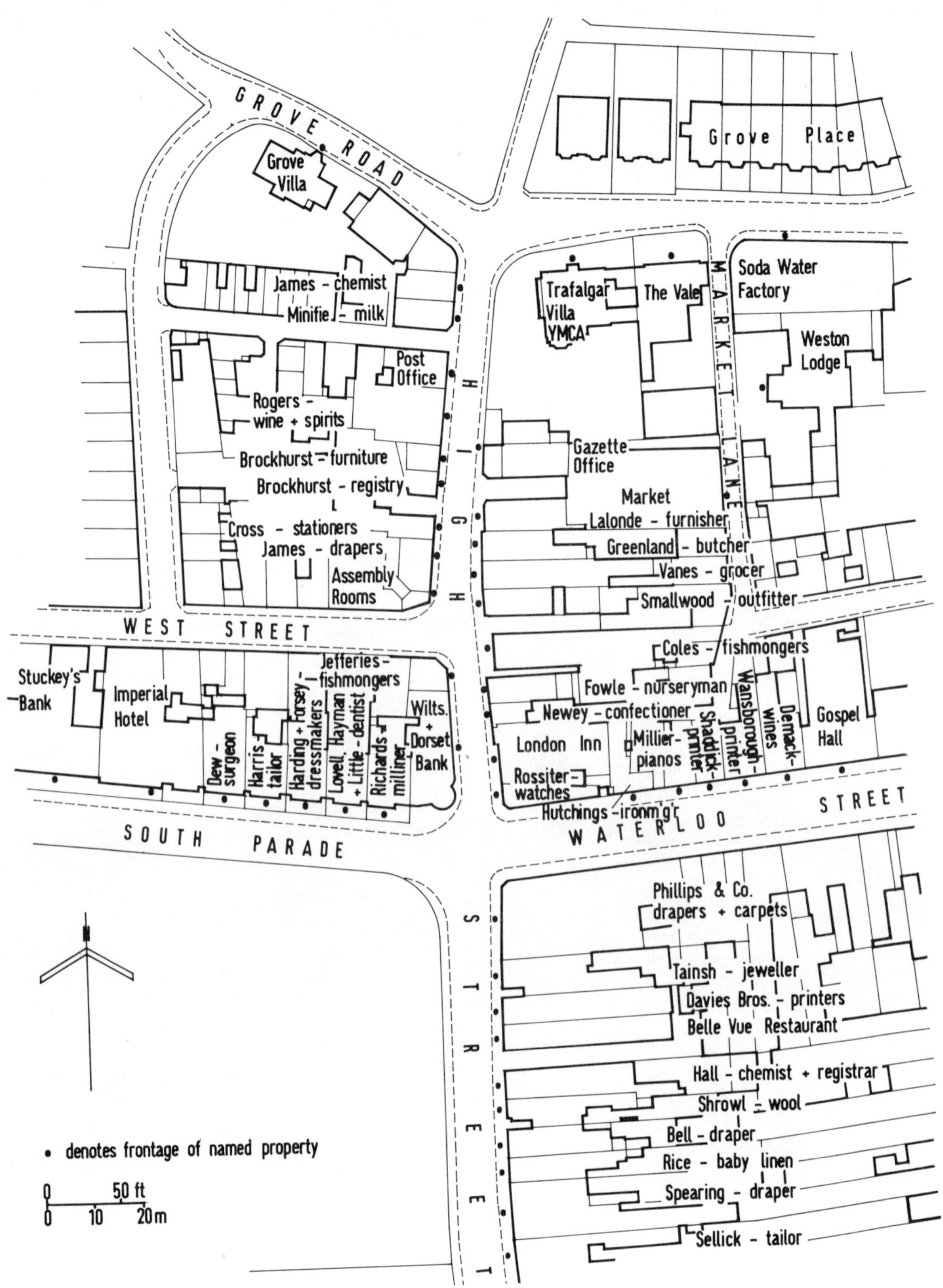

High Street shops in 1886.

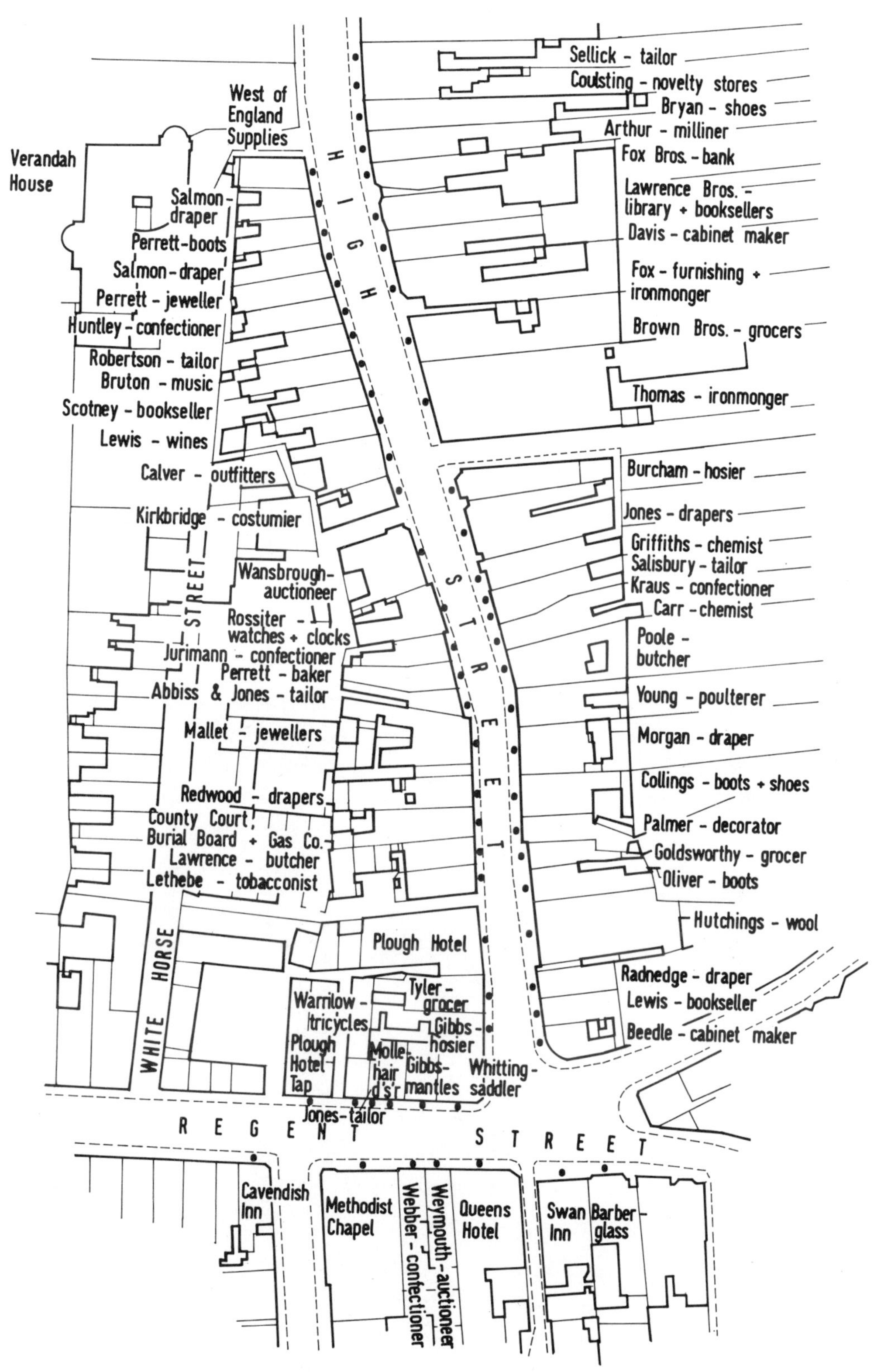

Sellick - tailor
Coulsting - novelty stores
Bryan - shoes
Arthur - milliner
Fox Bros. - bank
Lawrence Bros. - library + booksellers
Davis - cabinet maker
Fox - furnishing + ironmonger
Brown Bros. - grocers
Thomas - ironmonger
West of England Supplies
Verandah House
Salmon - draper
Perrett - boots
Salmon - draper
Perrett - jeweller
Huntley - confectioner
Robertson - tailor
Bruton - music
Scotney - bookseller
Lewis - wines
Calver - outfitters
Kirkbridge - costumier
HIGH STREET
Burcham - hosier
Jones - drapers
Griffiths - chemist
Salisbury - tailor
Kraus - confectioner
Carr - chemist
Poole - butcher
Young - poulterer
Morgan - draper
Collings - boots + shoes
Palmer - decorator
Goldsworthy - grocer
Oliver - boots
Hutchings - wool
Wansbrough - auctioneer
STREET
Rossiter - watches + clocks
Jurimann - confectioner
Perrett - baker
Abbiss & Jones - tailor
Mallet - jewellers
Redwood - drapers
County Court
Burial Board + Gas Co.
Lawrence - butcher
Lethebe - tobacconist
Plough Hotel
WHITE HORSE
Warrilow - tricycles
Tyler - grocer
Gibbs - hosier
Plough Hotel Tap
Molle hair d's'r
Gibbs - mantles
Whitting - saddler
Radnedge - draper
Lewis - bookseller
Beedle - cabinet maker
Jones - tailor
REGENT STREET
Cavendish Inn
Methodist Chapel
Webber - confectioner
Weymouth - auctioneer
Queens Hotel
Swan Inn
Barber - glass

SALE OF SHARES

IN THE

WESTON-SUPER-MARE

GAS-LIGHT COMPANY.

MR. E. G. LALONDE

HAS RECEIVED INSTRUCTIONS

TO SELL BY AUCTION

In pursuance and under the provisions of "The Weston-super-Mare Gas-Light Order, 1878,"

AT

LALONDE BROS.' AUCTION ROOMS, HIGH STREET,

WESTON-SUPER-MARE.

On Tuesday, the 16th day of June, 1896,

AT 6.30, FOR 7 O'CLOCK IN THE EVENING

150 SHARES

(Of the nominal Value of £20 each),

Class D

Of and in the above-mentioned Company issued under the provisions of the said Order.

The Shares will be Sold in Lots of not less than **Five Shares, or in such other Lots as may be determined on at the time of Sale.**

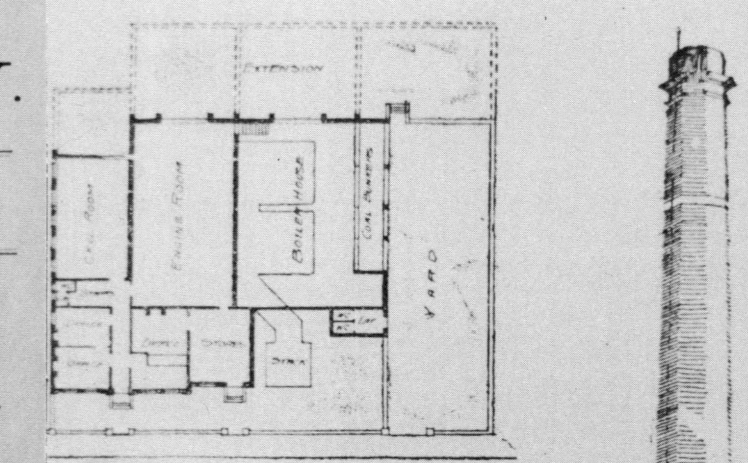

LEFT: Sale of share in the Gaslight Co in 1896 and RIGHT: the Electric Light station in 1910.

ABOVE: Glentworth Hall, built by the Cox family 1853/4, demolished 1973. (WM) BELOW left to right: Samuel Harvey, first Chairman of the UDC 1895-1897; the Borough crest in 1937 and Henry Butt, first Mayor of the Borough that year.

A street plan c 1900.

Anchor Head and the Marine Lake in 1978. (WAP)

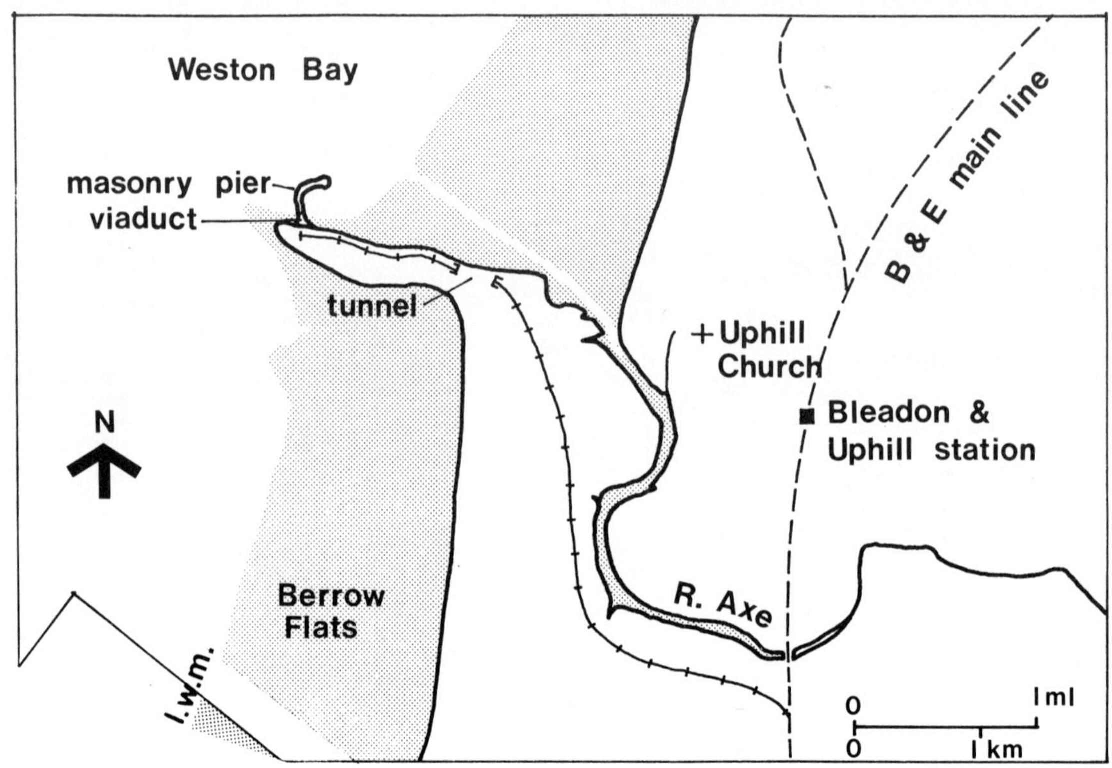

ABOVE: Dredges Pier, proposed 1845, never completed; CENTRE: Brean Down Harbour scheme, as proposed in 1864; BELOW: the scheme in 1861.

Promenades and Piers

The essence of any seaside resort is its sea front, and at Weston the sweep of the bay is complemented by a fine promenade stretching for over two miles. The main elements of the present front are the two piers, the buildings of Knightstone, the promenade and the beach lawns. These almost entirely Victorian and Edwardian creations are lasting monuments to many Westonians who put such considerable effort into their creation, and are worthy of special conservation.

Weston's long sandy beach had been its first promenade, used not only for walking but for riding and driving carriages along. The smooth surface was a great attraction for these latter pursuits in an age when the condition of most ordinary road surfaces was poor indeed. A low sea wall and gravelled promenade was made in the late 1820s between Knightstone and Regent Street and with little basic change this served the resort for fifty years. Its appearance was changed by the addition of many buildings, especially along the Knightstone Road, although the Hotel Field, now the site of the Winter Gardens, was protected by restrictive covenant and preserved the open aspect of the original promenade until the 1920s.

The promenade, the sands, Knightstone, and beyond the resort towards Uphill the long line of dunes, were easily able to accommodate even the much larger visitor numbers of the railway age, the dunes being a favourite picnic area for the many thousands of day visitors from Bristol. Thus the present sea front was not created because of overcrowding, but quite the reverse, for it is the result of a period of economic difficulty in the town that called for a drastic remedy. During the 1870s a combination of national economic recession (especially the beginning of what has been called the Great Victorian Depression in 1873) and rapid changes in holiday habits had produced problems for Weston. The seasons of 1877-9 were especially difficult, and the comment was made that the town had 'suffered pecuniarily from a diminution in the number of its visitors; and not only had the diminution been noticeable for many years past, but the social standing of the visitors was lower than in previous years'. It seems that many formerly regular visitors, especially those of higher social and economic standing, were seeking something different, and either travelled to Continental Europe or at least had moved their holiday haunts to the Devonshire coast. Torquay had perhaps the most impact upon Weston's share in the 'fashionable' visitor market, experiencing its most successful social development in the fifty years after 1840, since it remained isolated by distance from the 'tripper' crowds which were found increasingly at Weston.

Virtually the only alternative to further decline was to change quite radically the whole aesthetic basis of the resort, to offer the visitor something new and attract as staying visitors, rather than as trippers, the growing numbers of the lower classes who were just finding themselves able to afford a week by the sea. To change the public image of the resort was by no means an easy task, especially when faced with the drawbacks of an estuarine location, and that Weston was able to do this in a remarkably short space of time is a tribute to the considerable insight and political skill of a small group of local residents, notable among them Edwin Knight. Knight, who was the Chairman of the Commissioners, made the first moves to improvement when he outlined his views at a private dinner party in 1879. He advocated a massive improvement of the sea front, which was the very heart of the image of the resort carried home and retained in the memory of the visitor. Several of the Commissioners were convinced by Knight's arguments, enough to secure a majority in favour of setting up, on 3 December 1879, a committee to begin the necessary legal formalities. A further committee was appointed in January 1880 to prepare the plans in association with a consultant engineer from Bristol, T. J. Scoones.

After a year of preparatory work Edwin Knight stated that as far as he could see there was no reason why the scheme should not be started at once, and with the depression in the labour market and the large number of unemployed he thought the commencement of the scheme would not only prove a boon to the working classes but could also be carried out at a much cheaper rate than at any other time. However, the sea front scheme did not enjoy the approval of every inhabitant, even those such as John Gregory, a prominent local building contractor with direct financial interests in the prosperity of the town. With Gregory leading the opposition, a ratepayers' meeting came down strongly against the scheme, and this forced a Public Enquiry by the Local Government Board, the first ever held in Weston.

This took place in 1881, and the Inspector, S. J. Smith, heard extensive evidence from supporters and opposition. The opposition argument mainly seems to have been against any further social change in the resort. Colonel Turner, speaking on behalf of the local magistrates 'found that the advent of excursionists was very undesirable', and thought 'the scheme, if carried out, would only draw more excursionists, and not the class it was desirable to attract to the town'. The possibility of the dangerous driving of hired carriages by excursionists on the proposed carriage drive and the cost to the ratepayers were also cited, but possibly the most logical of the objections was that the scheme required the removal of the sand-hills bordering the beach, which were a popular attraction. The objectors with good reason asked if the substitute artificial gardens and lawns would really be preferred?

Only on the grounds of cost was the Inspector convinced by the opposition, and the scheme was sanctioned by the Local Government Board as originally proposed but without £3,000 worth of kiosks and ornamentation. After some legal difficulties had been overcome work could be started, and the foundation stone was laid by Cecil Hugh Smyth-Pigott on 15 March 1883. The scheme included the construction of new sea walls from Anchor Head to the Sanatorium, the removal of the dunes to the south of the town and creation of the present beach lawns, a boating slip at Anchor Head, new carriage drives and promenade, together with shelters, public conveniences and fencing. The whole work cost about £35,000, more than £2 per head of population, and required 1 million tons of stone, 85,000 cubic yards of earth filling, 9,000 yards of metalling, 49,000 yards of asphalting and 4,000 yards of running fencing. Most of the construction was carried out by Messrs A. Krauss of Bristol, although the boating slip was by H. A. Forse of Bristol and the adaptation of some buildings at Prince Consort Gardens for use as conveniences was by A. J. Marshall of Weston.

The major part of the front was complete by 1885, and by then it was obvious that this project had succeeded. A new feeling of confidence had been encouraged, resulting in a number of private investments which provided new amenities (the original Winter Garden and Pavilion in the Boulevard opened in 1882, and a fifteen acre recreation ground in 1885), while the very constructional activity had attracted more visitors. Combined with the much improved railway service on the loop line from 1884 it almost seemed as if a new resort had been created, and in 1886 the *Mercury* could comment that 'the local rates have fallen from 3s 6d to 3s in the pound since the expenditure on the sea front — despite the prophets of gloom in earlier days — the town has become fuller since the works were in hand'.

This renewed prosperity was based upon an increasing influx of excursionists and relatively short-stay visitors of the lower-middle and artisan classes, who were just beginning to gain holidays with pay. It is significant, for example, that in 1886 foremen at Wills' of Bristol tobacco factories had been given a week's holiday with pay, and in response to the demand Weston's speculative builders were building smaller boarding houses. Visitors from the industrial areas of South Wales, the Midlands and London as well as Bristol swelled the crowds, and even the *South Wales Echo* noted in 1888 that hotel proprietors and boarding-house keepers in Weston were welcoming this new class of 'staying excursionist' with open arms. Indeed, it considered that these were the people whose money 'made the "Mare" go for eight months in the year on the profits of the other four'. Weston had successfully made the transition into a more popular resort and into an era of further prosperity.

The sea front would not be complete today without its piers, and these too were important elements in the growth and development of Victorian and Edwardian Weston. The restrictions imposed by the tidal range precluded any extensive use of the Knightstone Wharf for the landing of passengers, and the small estuaries of the

Axe and Yeo rivers were too far from the resort to be of great use. Thus although by the early 1840s the 'cult of sea-trip going' had become firmly established in the Bristol Channel, Weston was missing much valuable trade by having no suitable landing place.

It had long been realised that Anchor Head was the most obvious place for a pier, since access to continuously navigable water was relatively easy, and it was this site which was chosen for the first pier. In April 1845 a committee was formed under the chairmanship of F. H. Synge to promote its construction, and following a public meeting a company was formed and shareholders obtained to provide the necessary capital. From small beginnings the ideas of this company soon expanded to include not only potential holiday traffic but to envisage the pier as a link in a major route for passengers and cargo between South Wales and the docks at Southampton and Portsmouth. To facilitate this a substantial pier consisting of a suspension bridge to Birnbeck Island and a landing pier extending into deep water beyond the island was designed by James Dredge, a Wiltshire engineer who had in 1836 been responsible for the Victoria Bridge over the Avon at Bath.

The necessary Parliamentary Act was passed in May 1846, Weston's church bells were rung in celebration, but money was short and work on the roadway and masonry suspension piers of the bridge did not begin until 1847. The project was then subject to the first of a series of difficulties from which it never really recovered; a masons' strike in July left work unfinished and this was damaged by the sea, then later in the year virtually the whole structure was destroyed in a storm. Neither Dredge nor the company had the finances to continue, and despite optimistic reports Dredge was declared bankrupt, owing the company £1,400 of which only £23 3s 11d could be paid back. The Pier Company was then wound up, leaving many of Weston's small businessmen investors with their fingers burned. The failure seems to have left a scar on the memory of many of them, who were for many years understandably reluctant to support pier projects with hard cash.

Despite numerous suggestions for piers, ranging in location from Sand Bay to Brean Down, and the opening for about a month of a floating pier at the mouth of the Axe in 1854, Weston was to remain without a pier until the 1860s. There were then two rival schemes, which eventually settled their differences to become firstly the Brean Down Harbour Company, which attempted unsuccessfully for nearly ten years to construct a commercial deep water harbour at the western end of Brean Down, and the Weston-super-Mare Pier Company, which successfully built the pier at Birnbeck. This latter company was largely the creation of the Smyth-Pigott estate, although attracting investment from businessmen in the town and elsewhere.

The laying of the foundation stone on 28 October 1864 by Master C. H. Smyth-Pigott was the occasion for a general holiday in Weston, and a dinner for 120 old people was given in the Assembly Rooms. The scheme then begun included the iron bridge from the mainland to Birnbeck that remains today, but also included a stone landing stage from the island to deep water, although this was later changed and an iron and wood landing stage, continuing the line of the bridge, was in fact constructed. The pier was designed by E. Birch, and erected by Messrs Toogoods from parts prefabricated at their Isca Foundry in Newport (Mon.). The bridge was completed by the end of 1866, and the pier, with its pavilion unfinished, opened on 5 June 1867. In its first three months of operation 120,000 people passed through the turnstiles, of which number it was said that '¾ were of the humbler class'. Receipts during this period totalled £5,000, but at the end of the summer the price of admission doubled to 2d, the first sign of difficult times ahead.

Indeed, although a new landing stage was built in 1872 funds were so short that the refreshment pavilion was not completed until the early 1880s, and the only extra attraction offered in the 1870s was a small 'plunge bath', opened in August 1872. There was no charge for using this bath between 6 am and 9 am! In fact the pier only became profitable during the 1880s, as the economy of Weston itself recovered from a depression. During 1883-84 an electric tramway was laid along the pier, the pavilion completed and the island paths asphalted. These improvements were followed by a gradual accumulation of funfair amusements, and by the early 1890s nearly 300,000 visited the pier each year, enabling the Pier Company to pay a record 9% dividend in 1892.

The response to such success was the initiation of further improvements in the landing facilities, as the paddle steamers of the Channel carried ever more passengers. In July 1898 a new jetty was added, and its completion was considered important enough to rate a three column front page lead story in the *Bristol Observer*, this alone showing that the pier had become one of the major attractions for the excursion visitor. Then in September 1903 there occurred the worst gale that Weston has known and both the new jetty and the landing stage were severely damaged. Indeed, much other damage was also caused in the town, Knightstone Causeway being partly washed away, causing the death of theatre electrician Edgar Bryant, smashing 50 bathing machines and there was considerable flooding. Even a massive counter in the Claremont Hotel was overturned by the sea breaking through. Fortunately both the town and the Pier soon recovered, and Harper was able to comment of the pier in 1909 that here were 'such dreams of delight . . . . that many venture no further: water-chutes, switchback railways, try your weight and strength machines, and, above all, a damned something that may be espied from the shore, like a giant's stride pole with baskets filled with people who paid 1d to be given a good imitation of sea sickness'. However, by then the Birnbeck Pier had competition, but through good fortune managed to maintain its monopoly of steamer services and, until the 1930s, a virtual monopoly of the popular mechanical amusements as well. It has even played a part in military history, for as 'HMS Birnbeck' during the 1939-45 War it was used for the testing of a number of new weapons for the Royal Navy.

However, Birnbeck was peripheral to the main concentration of resort activity in Weston. Although the pier and its vicinity were often thronged during the busy public holidays it was clear that many of the train-borne visitors were not prepared to move from the beach near Regent Street, while those arriving by steamer contributed little or nothing to the town's economy. It was with this division of the excursion visitors in mind that scarcely a decade after the completion of the first, discussions began about a new pier on a new site. An easy solution presented itself — why not build a pier which was in effect an extension across to navigable water of the main excursionist thoroughfare, Regent Street itself? This was the idea adopted by the new pier interests in the late 1870s and publicly announced in the spring of 1880.

Once more it was money that caused the main problem, for although detailed proposals were made and an Act of Parliament obtained in 1884, the project had to be abandoned in 1885 through lack of support. Then during the 1890s the scheme was revived, together with other suggestions for piers from Knightstone Island and from the proposed Glentworth Bay enclosing wall. The latter was supported by the Urban District Council and formed part of an Act which it was obtaining in 1896. However the Council was not allowed to proceed with its pier proposals, and the field was left free for the private company to construct the Grand Pier. £200,000 was subscribed, mainly by people in Weston and Cardiff, and work began on 7 November 1903. By the following summer the contractors, Mayoh and Haley of London, had completed the pavilion and first stage of the pier and these were opened on 11 June 1904. A further 1,500 feet of pier with a wooden landing stage were added in 1905, making a total length of 2,580 feet, which was less than half the length anticipated in the original design. This was unfortunate, for the reduced length necessitated by financial constraints meant that the pier was almost an instant failure as a passenger landing place. It was badly affected by currents, and its actual construction seems to have added to the silting problem. Only three steamers attempted to call, the first severely damaging the landing stage and the others did little better. The approach channel rapidly silted up, and thereafter pleasure steamer captains refused to call there.

The Grand Pier was, nevertheless, a great asset to Weston. A variety of entertainment was provided in the Pavilion theatre, from Band Concerts to Shakespeare's plays, which were popular but not lucrative enough to stop the original company going into liquidation in 1919. Meanwhile during the First World War the low water extension was demolished, leaving the pier at its present length. A new company, headed by the Marquis of Bute, took over in 1919, and continued the previous entertainment policy with success until the Pavilion burnt down in a spectacular fire in January 1930. In order to cut their losses, for the insurance would have covered only half the cost of rebuilding, the company then sold the pier to Leonard Guy, who had previously held the sideshow concessions.

He built the present pavilion, and established, against much local opinion, the large indoor funfair which has remained a feature of Weston to this day.

Although the Urban District Council was unable to include a pier in its late 19th century programme of improvements, it nevertheless took an active part in the development of the sea front amenities. The most important of its actions was the purchase of Knightstone Island in 1896. Since the 1830s there had been a number of changes on the island, most notably the building of a covered ladies' swimming bath in the 1880s. However it had seldom been a profitable operation, and in 1891 the new owners, 'Knightstone Weston-super-Mare Ltd', applied to increase the commercial use of the wharf, which was then seeing the import of about 20,000 tons of coal a year (all unloaded from beached sloops to carts on the beach). The UDC was not in favour of such commercial development, and it was almost inevitable that it should purchase the island, since no other local source of capital could be found to provide the badly needed new holiday amenities. It cost £13,482.

In fact the purchase was part of an extensive plan of improvement drawn up by the engineers Wolfe-Barry and Brereton, which unfortunately could not be carried through because of financial difficulties. Only the works on Knightstone were carried out, consisting of the present theatre and new covered swimming baths, both of which were opened in 1902, adding significantly to Weston's visitor amenities for the 20th century.

The Wolfe-Barry and Brereton plans' other provisions, which included the enclosure of Glentworth Bay by a barrage, (later undertaken as part of an unemployment relief programme and completed in 1929) were concerned with a problem which had beset Weston throughout its career as a resort — the large expanse of mud exposed every day when the tide retreated. The earliest guide book came to terms with this by emphasising the delights to be experienced when the tide came in again, while later in the 19th century came the idea that 'ozone' created by the mud was 'good for you'. Then in the 1920s this deft piece of calculation appeared in the official guide:

'Estimating the area of Weston Bay at 2,500 acres, there occurs four times a day an average displacement of 4,000 million cubic feet of air in front of the town, which of itself ensures a change and purification of the atmosphere of Weston in even the calmest weather and adds greatly to the salubrity of the climate.'

This was almost an admission of defeat, but there had been a number of ideas for creating barrages across the bay to retain permanent water at the edge of the sands. Proposals for enclosing Glentworth Bay came as early as 1871, and were raised several times in the 1880s. A scheme for a 500 by 150 yard marine lake on the sands between Ellenborough and Clarence Parks was published by J. S. Whittington in 1888, and a company was even floated to undertake its construction. As always there was insufficient finance, but this did not deter the UDC adopting the Wolfe-Barry and Brereton scheme in 1895 which advocated enclosing not only Glentworth Bay but most of Weston Bay from Knightstone to Black Rock at Uphill. As we have seen, only the enclosure of Glentworth was accomplished, but with current proposals for a Severn Barrage, Weston may yet see its tidal problem solved. It is to be hoped that this will not result in a permanent state of half-tide, as some current plans suggest, as if so then once again Weston might have to invest in a new sea front, at rather more expense to the ratepayer than the prices of the 1880s.

Birnbeck Pier in the 1890's.

LEFT: Mr Brookes, Pier Master, Birnbeck Pier 1893; RIGHT: Cecil Hugh Smyth Pigott (1860-1893). He laid the foundation stone of Birnbeck Pier in 1864 and that of the new sea front in 1883. (WM) BELOW: The Pier as it should have looked at its 1867 opening — but the Pavilion was not ready.

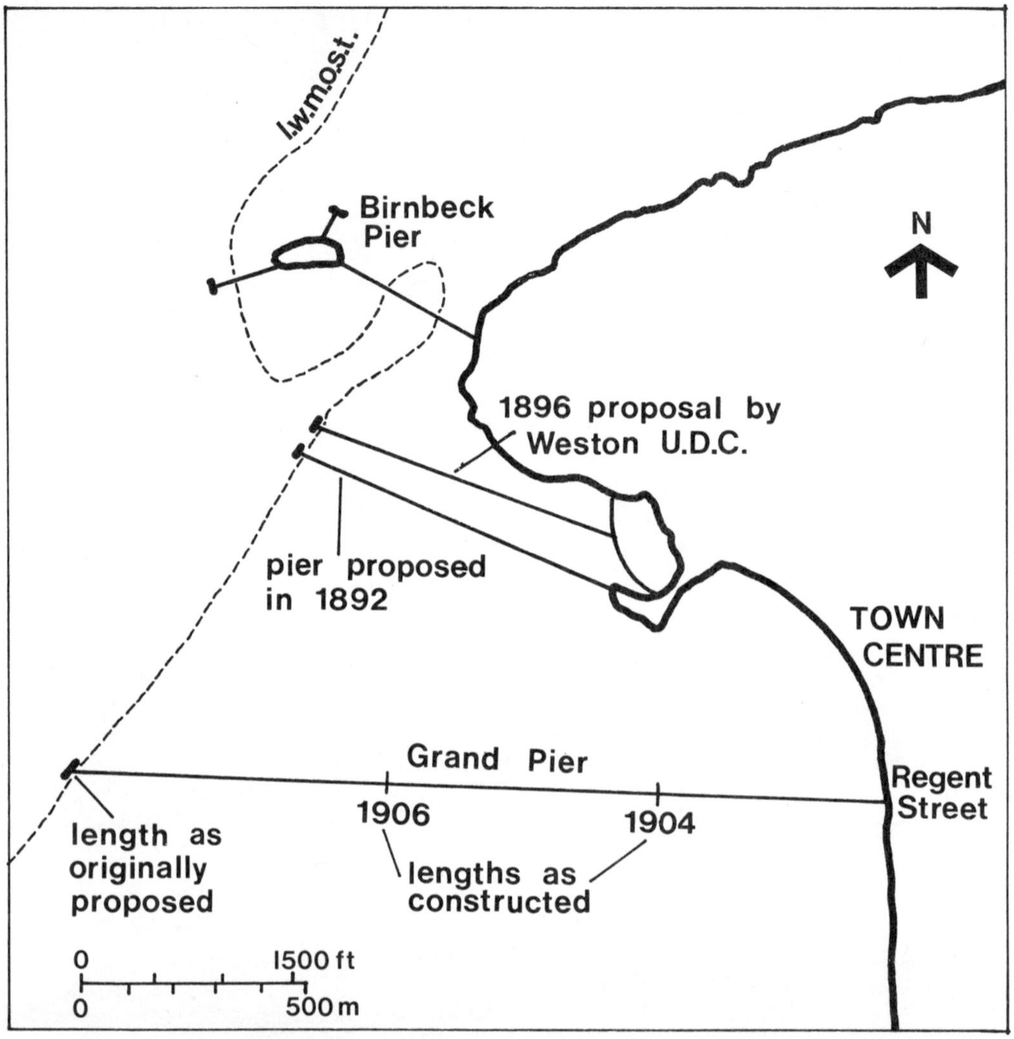

l.w.m.o.s.t.

Birnbeck Pier

N

1896 proposal by Weston U.D.C.

pier proposed in 1892

TOWN CENTRE

Grand Pier

Regent Street

1906

1904

length as originally proposed

lengths as constructed

0 1500 ft

0 500 m

ABOVE: The pier proposals of the 1890's and 1900's and BELOW: Beach Lawns, c 1910.

ABOVE: Banqueting Hall, Birnbeck Pier, 1893 and BELOW: the Pier c 1910.

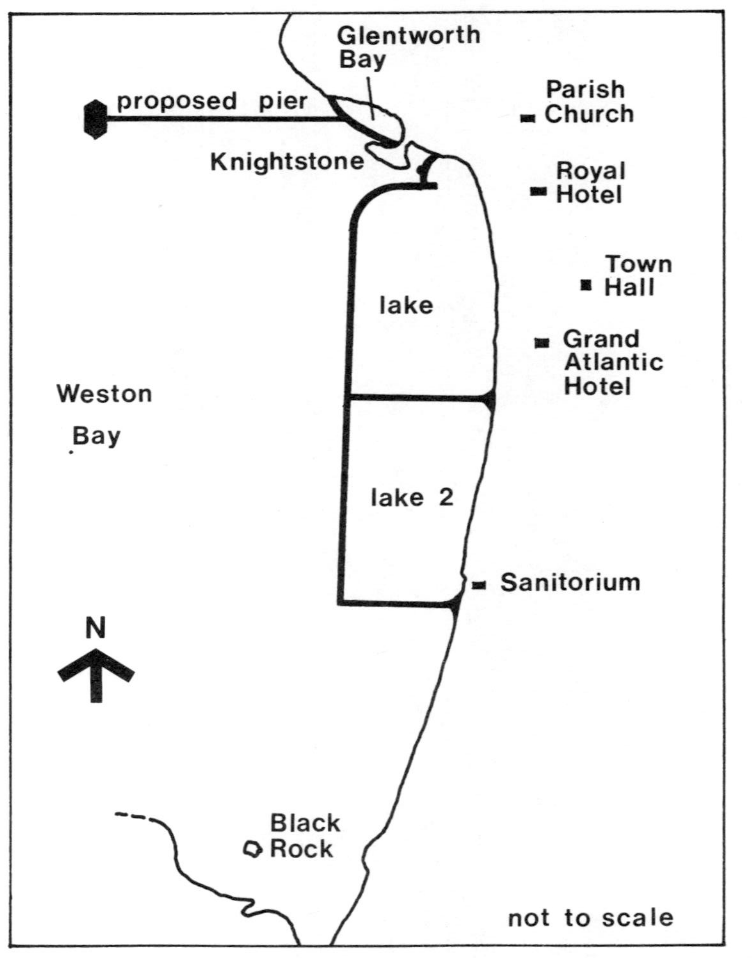

LEFT: The Marine Lake and Pier proposals by Wolfe-Barry and Brereton, 1895 and RIGHT: facilities advertised in 1910.

Grand Pier, ABOVE: foundation piles, 1903, CENTRE: under construction that same year and BELOW: the Pavilion, burnt down in 1930.

ABOVE: Grand Pier in 1933 and BELOW: Glentworth Bay before the enclosure of the Marine Lake.

ABOVE: Prince Consort Gardens and Birnbeck Pier in the 1920's and BELOW: the Water Shute at the Pier.

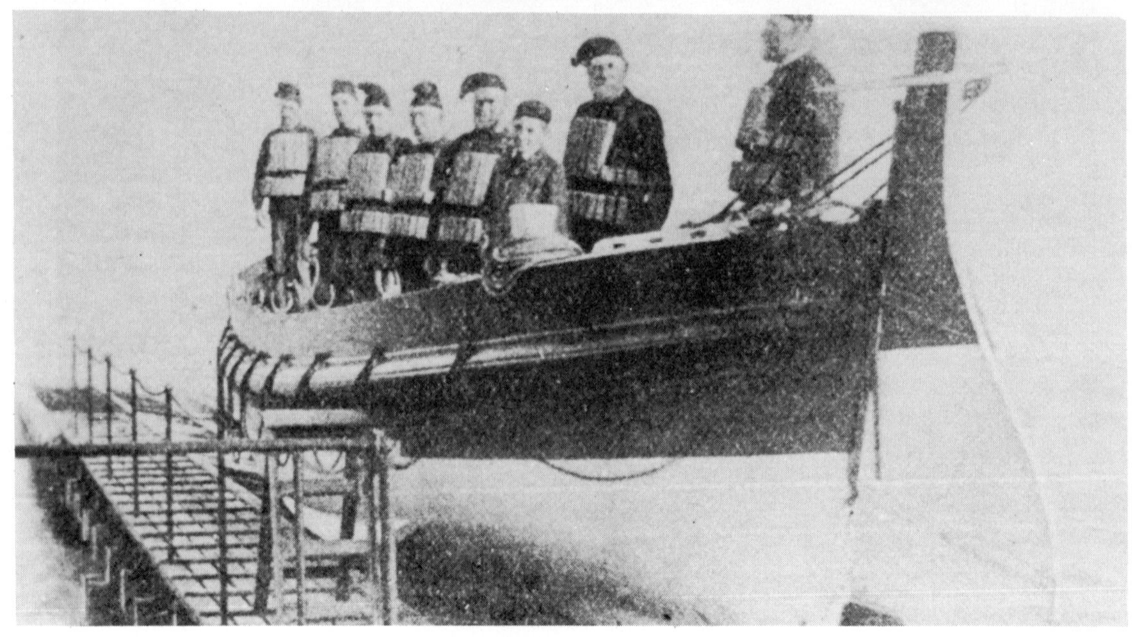

ABOVE: Weston's first lifeboat, CENTRE: the crew in 1881 and BELOW: another early lifeboat.

LEFT: Cycling Club outing, c 1890, RIGHT: building the Marine Lake in 1928 and BELOW: in 1930.

ABOVE: Weston-super-Mare from on high in 1928 and BELOW: on the beach in the 1920's.

ABOVE: The model yacht pond and BELOW: racing there in the 1920's and RIGHT: Diana Fluck, (Diana Dors), 3rd prizewinner in 'Miss Modern Venus' 1945.

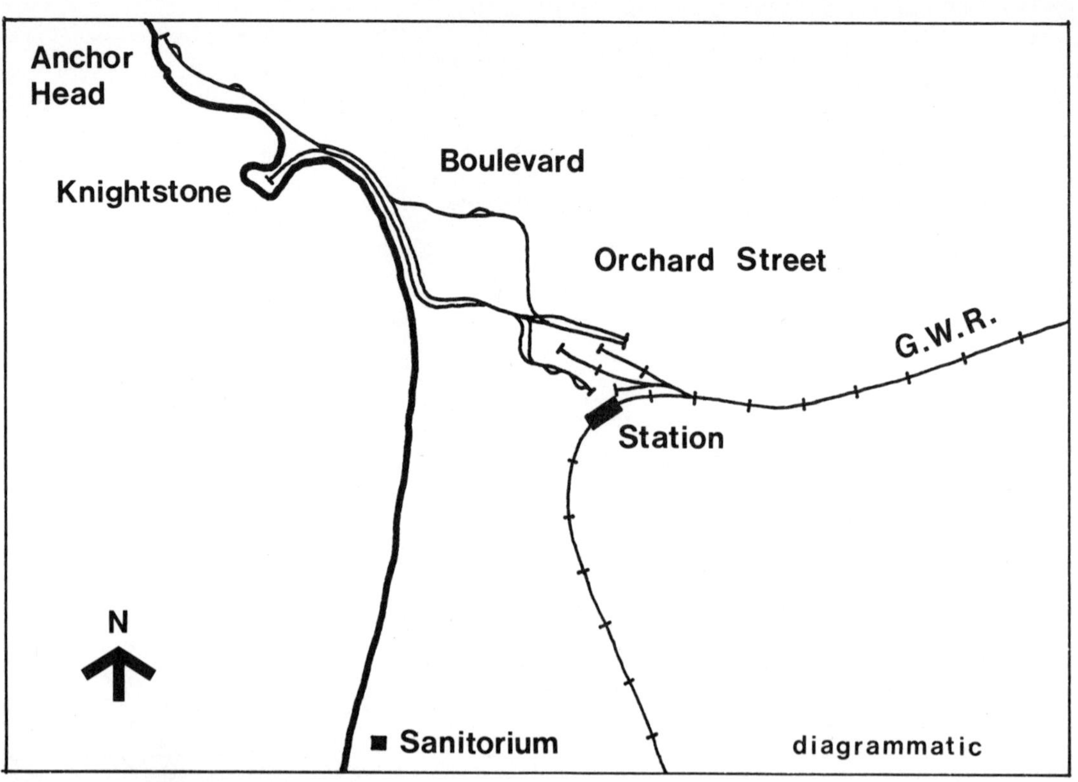

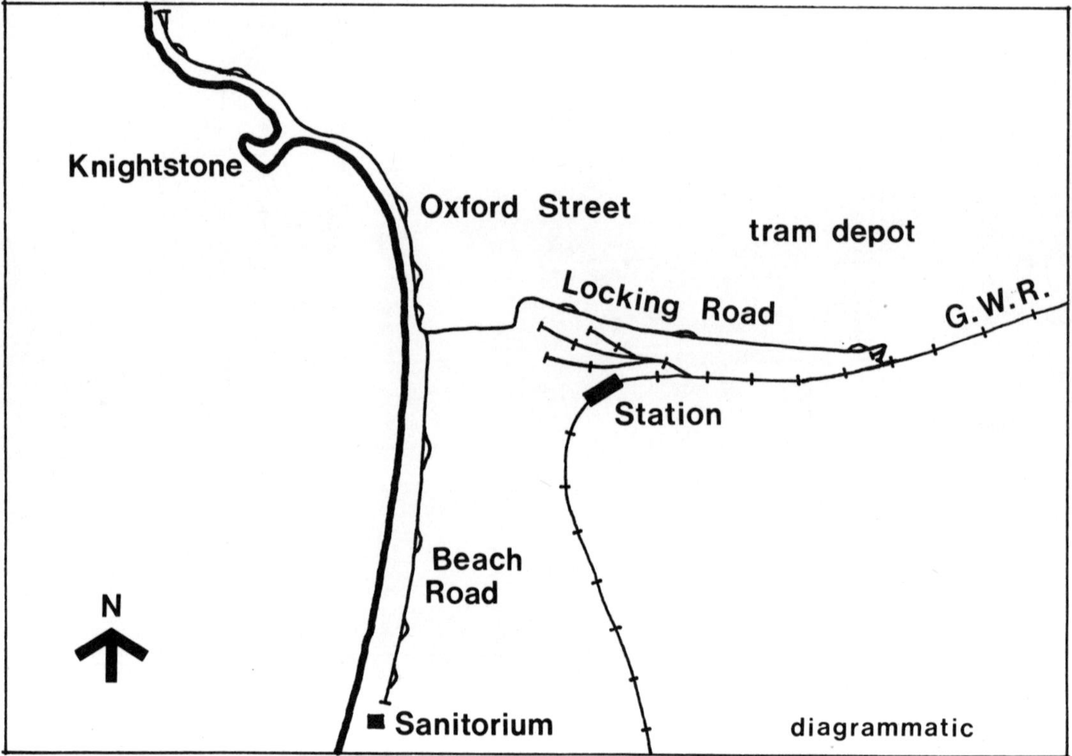

The tramway system ABOVE: proposed in 1886, and BELOW: completed in 1902.

Transports of Delight

Even from its earliest days as a resort Weston has offered to the visitor many opportunities to explore the town and its surroundings in ease and comfort. The Guide Book of 1822 mentioned that 'jaunting cars, wheel and sedan chairs, ponies and donkies' could be hired, and there were many enterprising inhabitants who entered the transport trade. By the 1850s the town was well provided with carriages of all types, and excursions to places of interest such as the caves at Cheddar had become commonplace. Probably the most popular outing was the round trip to Worle and Kewstoke, returning via the Toll Road to Weston. Tea could be taken at one of the villages *en route* and an afternoon outing of this sort would have cost only about 1s 6d. Within the town, visitors were able to hire horse-drawn cabs for journeys to and from the station, while the so-called 'twopenny brakes' provided a popular service along the sea front from the Royal Hospital to the Old Pier.

For the majority the greatest impact upon their holiday mobility was made by the development of public transport, especially Weston's trams, the Weston, Clevedon and Portishead Light Railway, and more recently the extensive 'bus and coach services. Interest in the building of a street tramway system began in 1872, when the Pier Company was involved in a proposal to connect the two main points of excursionist arrival, its own Pier and the railway station, in an effort to attract more visitors to the Birnbeck area. There was a good deal of support for this proposal, and it was rejected by the Local Board by the margin of only one vote on the grounds of noise and traffic hazard. An unsuccessful attempt was made to revive this scheme in 1878, then in 1886 another and more elaborate plan was published for a system which would have served virtually the whole town. Once again no capital could be raised, and the project was abandoned.

There was obviously potential for a service however, and late in the century the Weston, Clevedon and Portishead Light Railway Company obtained powers to lay a street tramway to the Boulevard as an extension of its main line. Track was in fact laid along Gerard Road and the Boulevard in 1897, but an objection was raised by the Urban District Council because, it claimed, the rails stood above the road surface and were dangerous. The Company replied that it was not prepared to use any other type of rail (it was too short of money to undertake expensive alterations), and since it did not even repay the Council for road repair work which it had itself failed to do, the track was lifted and the whole scheme abandoned before any services had run. At this time other moves were afoot, and three years later the Weston-super-Mare and District Electric Supply Company (a part of the British Electric Traction group) obtained a Tramways Order for 3.71 miles of line.

Only 2.92 miles of track were actually laid, the proposed lines in Milton Road and Station Road not being constructed, and the first electric tram ran on 12 May 1902. The system itself was simple, consisting of a line along the Locking Road leading from the depot (now the site of the S.W.E.B. offices and workshops), through Oxford Street to the most important and well used track which was that running along the entire length of the sea front. Throughout, the track was single with numerous passing loops, current being obtained from overhead wires.

For a small system it was remarkably successful, carrying an average of 1.46 million passengers per year, most of these being holidaymakers travelling on the sea front route — often on the 'toast rack' single deck open-sided trams, although the system also ran'winter cars' which had an open top deck and covered downstair accommodation, each with seats for 35 passengers. Despite early and quite strong resentment on the part of Weston's cab drivers and donkeymen, who even resorted to the obstruction of trams by deliberately slow driving, the system soon became an accepted feature. It also influenced the linear spread of housing along and beyond its Locking Road route, while making the select estate developments at Clarence Park and along Uphill Road more accessible to the town centre.

Omnibus services on two sea front routes, using horse-drawn vehicles, had begun during 1890 but here were no regular 'bus services in Weston until 1912. Then during the 1920s strong competition developed between 'buses and trams. Hampered by the restrictions of its single track and the high cost of any extensions to the system the tramway was unable to compete, and following purchase by the Bristol Tramways and Carriage Company it was closed on 17 April 1937. Few traces of the trams now remain, and even the records of its operations have been either lost or destroyed.

The same is true of the Weston-super-Mare, Clevedon and Portishead Light Railway, a line with a short but extremely colourful history and still fondly remembered by many local residents. During the 19th century the absence of any direct links with Weston's coastal neighbours Clevedon and Portishead had frequently been noted, and in 1880 James Collings of Weston put forward a plan for a coastal road to Clevedon. The road plan gained little support, but it perhaps inspired the idea of a light railway along the coast, and thus in 1885 the privately sponsored Weston, Clevedon and Portishead Tramways Bill received Royal Assent. Both Clevedon and Weston interests lay behind this tramway, whose directors included Sir Edward Elton of Clevedon and two prominent Weston solicitors, Samuel Baker and Henry Wansbrough. After struggling to raise the necessary capital, public services between Weston and Clevedon began on 1 December 1897, after which 'the tramway quickly got into its stride, and special late trains were run between Clevedon and Weston on 21st December in connection with a meat and poultry show at the latter town'. During its first year of operation the line carried 282,000 passengers, many of them holidaymakers, and had a considerable impact, expecially upon trade at Clevedon.

The line was extended to Portishead in the early part of the present century, opening on 7 August 1907, but only after more financial difficulties and complaints about the routing and dangers of the line in Clevedon, where there were awkward road crossings. The railway carried some mineral traffic from local quarries to the GWR junction at Portishead, and from its wharf at Wick St Lawrence coal was taken to Clevedon gasworks, but its principal income was from holidaymakers. With its rather quaint locomotive stock, variety of passenger coaches (including some early ones originally destined for South America), the unimportance of the timetable and friendly atmosphere the line soon entered local folklore, but was seldom able to make a profit. Although today a railway such as this could not fail to be an overwhelming success, during the 1930s the impact of the motor car and improved 'bus services was too great, and the line closed on 18 May 1940.

In Weston itself, the 20th century saw the rapid growth of both 'bus and coach services. In 1905 there was only one motor coach for hire in Weston, a 28 hp Daimler brake capable of carrying ten passengers, but the number of 'charabancs' increased rapidly and by 1911 charabanc trips were running as far afield as Cheddar and Glastonbury. During the following year the Bristol Tramways and Carriage Company introduced the first regular 'bus service, curiously known as 'No. 40', running from Ashcombe Park to Uphill Park Estate, and soon after began a Bristol to Weston-super-Mare service. Rapid expansion followed the Great War, with many new town and country services developed under the guiding hand of J. D. Howell, the local manager for 30 years from 1921. By the 1930s the services merited a large new 'bus station, and the present Beach Bus Station opened in 1936.

Finally, Weston also became interested in aviation, partly because of its publicity value in the early decades of the 20th century. It was even suggested that an aviation week be held during 1910, although the first aeroplane seen in the town did not arrive until 1911. This was piloted by Colonel S. F. Cody, who landed on the beach opposite the Grand Atlantic Hotel during August Bank Holiday week. Later that year, on 1 September, B. C. Hucks made history by making the first flight across the Bristol Channel, a return trip to Cardiff and Newport from Weston. However, exhibition flights such as those given by Hucks, later 'flying circus' visits, and even pleasure flights from the beach near the Royal Hospital, are only part of the town's aviation history. During the 1930s the Council decided to open a municipal airport, and this was constructed on land at Locking Moor in 1936. Initially its commercial flights to Cardiff and Birmingham were successful, with 36,000 passengers handled in the first year of operation. Proximity to Bristol Airport and the relatively short runway limited development however, and following military use during the war the Airport became mainly a base for amenity flying. It is now restricted to private flying and use for the sport of gliding.

BOARD OF TRADE: SESSION 1887

Weston-super-Mare Tramways.

NOTICE IS HEREBY GIVEN that on or before the 23rd day of December, 1886, application will be made to the Board of Trade for a Provisional Order to authorise the laying down of certain street Tramways and that it is proposed to lay one or more or some part or parts of such Tramways along the street or road, or part of the street or road in which this notice is posted.

Plans of the Tramways proposed to be authorised by the Provisional Order will, on or before the 30th day of November instant, be deposited at the office of the Clerk of the Parliaments, House of Lords, at the Private Bill Office of the House of Commons, at the Railway Department of the Board of Trade, with the Clerk of the Peace for the County of Somerset at his office at Wells, with the Clerk to the Local Board of Weston-super-Mare at his office at Weston-super-Mare, with the Clerk to the Urban Sanitary Authority of Weston-super-Mare at his office at Weston-super-Mare, and with the Clerk of the Parish of Weston-super-Mare at his residence.

Dated this 14th day of November, 1886.

BAKER, SON, JAMES & REED,
Weston-super-Mare,
Solicitors.

C. J. HANLY & CO.,
2, Princes Street, Great George Street,
Westminster, S.W.
Parliamentary Agents.

Notice of application to the Board of Trade for permission to lay a tramway in 1886.

ABOVE: Toastrack tram of the 1930's, BELOW: 'bus competition and INSET: a tram ticket.

The Subscription List will be closed on or before Thursday, May 27th.

THE

WESTON-SUPER-MARE, CLEVEDON & PORTISHEAD (STEAM) TRAMWAYS COMPANY,

(With Junctions with the Great Western Railway.)

Incorporated by special Act of Parliament 48 and 49 Vict. Cap. 182, whereby the liability of each Shareholder is absolutely limited to the amount unpaid on his Subscription.

CAPITAL £60,000 IN 6,000 SHARES OF £10 EACH.

Payable £1 on application, £1 on allotment, and the balance in calls not exceeding £2, at intervals of not less than two months.

Directors:

Until the First Meeting of the Company.

SIR EDMUND HARRY ELTON, BART., Chairman, Clevedon Court, Somerset.
SAMUEL EDWARD BAKER, Esq., Weston-super-Mare.
HENRY DANIEL, Esq., Tyndalls Park, Clifton.
JOHN GRIFFIN, Esq., Kenn, Somerset.
HENRY WANSBROUGH, Esq., Weston-super-Mare.

Engineer:

F. C. STILEMAN, Esq., C.E., Great George Street, Westminster.

Solicitors:

Messrs. OSB[illegible] [illegible]RD, VASSALL [illegible]

ABOVE: The Tram Depot in Locking Road and BELOW: a prospectus to raise capital for the WCPLR in 1886.

ABOVE: WCPLR engine *CLEVEDON* in 1900 and BELOW: WCPLR engine *WESTON* with a train, crossing the Yeo river in 1899. INSET: a direction sign. (WM)

ABOVE: Traffic jam on Locking Road in the 1950's; BELOW: a coach tour of 1924 and RIGHT: poster for an exhibition flight by B.C. Hucks on 1 September, 1911.

Weston at Work

Weston's holiday visitors provided the market for many trades, crafts and public utilities throughout the 19th century, and although the resort could by no means have been described as an industrial town in that period there were many interesting manufacturing and service occupations. During the present century, and especially since 1939, the town has also experienced considerable growth in employment over a much wider industrial field until today such activities must be of nearly equal importance to the holiday trades.

During the 19th century the largest of the trades was that of building, which included the largest single employers (for example in 1871 F. Date, who was then the largest contractor, employed over 100 men), and the greatest proportion of the town's itinerant labour force. However, since the rate of building varied greatly from year to year, the building trade was not able to offer stable employment, and these variations also caused problems for the local manufacturers of bricks and tiles. Stemming from such insecurity, and combined with the need for considerable investment in plant for this industry, it is not surprising that the opportunity for diversification was taken, producing not only Weston's largest 19th century manufacturing industry but a concern which served a national market, namely the Royal Potteries.

The manufacture of bricks, tiles and various types of domestic pottery ware probably began in Weston during the 1820s, when the first major phase of building was taking place. Good reserves of clay were available on land which was not then required for building. Documentary evidence for the early industry is lacking, but by 1836 one brickworks had certainly been established alongside Locking Road by William Wilcox, and by 1843 it had been joined by another enterprise on an adjoining site. It is believed that these two businessmen continued to operate individual concerns until about 1860, when, due to lack of clay reserves, Wilcox transferred his operations to a site at Banwell where he continued trading successfully, and during the 1880s also leasing the Strode Road brickworks from the Elton family of Clevedon. But it was the other brickworks and pottery, probably begun by Samuel Searle, which grew to become the Royal Potteries.

Charles Phillips, who was born, probably in Weston, in about 1827, was the intelligent but illiterate man who made the Royal Potteries into a significant enterprise. At the age of nine he was already acquiring the potter's skills, and by

1843 he was in business making red ware pottery at the New Inn, Gas Street. Shortly afterwards he began working at the newer of the two Locking Road works, and was able to purchase the firm in 1847. Realising that the local clay deposits produced flower pots of excellent porosity, Phillips began to expand the production of these for both domestic and horticultural use, for they yielded much greater returns per pound of clay than bricks, and were not subject to comparable variations in demand. By the use of advertising, and by exhibiting his wares at many horticultural shows the sales of his pots rose rapidly. At the Great Exhibition in the Crystal Palace in 1851 they received an 'Honourable Mention', and laid the basis for national sales.

At this time the pottery was still dependent upon its brick output and in 1855 a recession in the building trade during installation of new plant bankrupted Phillips. The pottery and its stock were auctioned in November of that year, but by the following April he was back in control, apparently rescued by the Pigott estate in the interests of maintaining its own brick supply. Phillips was retained as manager, and was later able to buy back the business. Thus it was under Phillips' guidance that prosperity returned, and orders for the Royal Parks enabled him to describe the business as 'under Royal Patronage'; soon after he adopted the 'Royal Pottery' title. In the later 1850s and 1860s he introduced many new types of pots and a wide range of garden ornaments, and sales rose rapidly. In 1862 when the new goods station opened the first loads to be dispatched were three wagons of pots for a London customer.

In 1871 the Pottery was bought by John Matthews, who continued its prosperity by expanding still further the range of extraordinarily detailed and complex flowerpots, busts of William Shakespeare, figures of Punch, dogs, lions and many similar products. Quite a number of these are still to be seen in Weston gardens. These items were made in addition to vast numbers of standard pots by a workforce of perhaps 40 or 50, who kept the six kilns on the Locking Road site in fairly constant use. The *Gardeners' Chronicle and Agricultural Gazette* of 1872 stated that the pottery produced about 1½ million pots per year, making it the largest single production unit of its kind in the United Kingdom. All the pots were thrown individually on wheels until the successful introduction of plaster moulding methods in the 1930s.

Conway G. Warne, a potter from Rochester in Kent, took over the Potteries in 1884. By this time the Victorian fashion for ornamental pots was waning, and Warne proved himself another inventive potter by patenting several new products. The first of these, in 1884, was a land drain well, followed by an electric cable trough which was used in Bristol, Sale, Hampstead and Weston itself. Roofing tile manufacture was also increased, while the standard flowerpots remained in production, the *Ironmonger's Chronicle* reporting in 1893 that they were in use in all the London Parks.

At the end of the century clay reserves on the Locking Road site were at an end, and the pottery moved to a new location off Winterstoke Road in 1900. The old site was rapidly phased out, and since the old clay pits had for some time been used for dumping the town's refuse, the area was soon developed for housing, leaving no surface trace of the old works. During the present century the pottery experienced mixed fortunes, struggling to survive until eventual closure in 1914. It re-opened after the war mainly for brick making in Weston's 1920s building boom, then reverted to flowerpot making in the 1930s. Using the new moulding techniques it then became once again one of the country's major manufacturers. Bricks, tiles and flowerpots continued to be made until 1961, when the company went into voluntary liquidation, beaten by the rise of the plastic flowerpot.

Virtually all other significant employment in 19th century Weston was in industries and utilities having close links with the holiday visitors and leisured residents. It was mainly to supply visitors with the sort of advanced facilities they were probably just becoming used to in their own homes that the Weston Gasworks was begun in 1841. A small plant costing £2,500 was erected in Gas Street, apparently occupying the same building as the town's original Police Station. It was said to have supplied gas at a cost of ½ guinea per 1,000 cubic feet to 50 consumers, and provided for 42 street lamps.

Under the provisions of the 1842 Improvement Act the local Commissioners leased the Gasworks, considering that this would enable them to provide street lighting in the most economical way. The arrangement proved unsatisfactory, for the works were too small to cater for a growing town, and in 1851 the lease was terminated, for the Commissioners had no wish to invest in the necessary new plant. The Gas Company themselves then added some new equipment, and raised the price of the gas to finance it — but the Commissioners refused to pay the increase and as a result Weston was without street lighting during the winter of 1853-54.

Soon after the disagreement had been settled it was decided to build a completely new works outside the town to avoid the smells and pollution caused by the original site. Horatio Parsley gave the land next to the branch railway line adjoining Drove Road, and the new works opened in 1856. Major expansions took place in 1915 and 1937 as the Gas Company extended its supply area over much of Somerset, but these have been swept away since production ceased in 1968. Today only a few of the earliest buildings survive on the Drove Road site, now occupied by South West Gas. In 1913 the Gas Company built a large block of offices and stores in Burlington Street, and this impressive building has now been most successfully transformed into the town's museum.

Apart from the waterworks, the public utility picture in Weston was completed by the opening of a small electricity generating station in 1901. This was run by a subsidiary of the British Electric Traction Company called the Weston-super-Mare and District Electric Supply Company. The generating station was on Locking Road, the site also being used as the tramway depot. Little trace of the former generating plant now remains, for with the development of grid systems the need for the many small stations of Weston's type disappeared, and the site is now used as offices and depot by the South Western Electricity Board.

Although it is impossible here to list in detail the large number of small industrial units, craftsmen and traders who were at work in and around Weston in the 19th century, some of the more important deserve consideration. Not surprisingly many of these small enterprises were concerned with the food and drink requirements of the visitors and residents, and undoubtedly the Worle Brewery and Ross and Company were the major representatives of this group. The brewery at Worle was established on a site at the junction of Worle High Street and what is now Station Road in 1795 by James May in partnership with a Mr Castle. It was a small but lasting business which supplied the local area until it was put up for sale by the sons of the original proprietors in 1865. It was purchased by the 'Weston-super-Mare Brewing & Malting Company', which was largely the creation of the Weston solicitor Henry Davis. Much new equipment was installed during 1867, but Davis died before brewing restarted and the company was wound up in 1868. Many of the local inns had been supplied by the brewery and they had to look elsewhere for beer, obtaining deliveries from several of the larger regional breweries which were established at that time. The brewery buildings stood empty until 1879 when they were converted into a laundry.

The manufacture of various types of aerated 'mineral' water dated from the 1770s, but its production in Weston did not begin until the 1850s, and only reached substantial proportions in the 1870s. In 1869 William M. Forty acquired the 'Weston and West of England Soda Manufactory' whose small premises were located in Orchard Street. Trading under the name of 'Ross and Company' Mr Forty successfully increased his trade and in 1880 moved to larger premises in Lower Bristol Road (later occupied by Grove Park garage and now Knightstone House flats). He also opened branch factories in Barnstaple and Newport, and his products were said to have had a wide international distribution — certainly they were sent as far afield as Aden and Peru. In addition soft drinks were made by at least two other concerns, John Parrett and H. T. George of the Westwick Brewery, Worle, established in 1863, and W. G. Carpenter at the rear of 73 George Street, established in 1898.

The impact of the large regional breweries was paralleled in the present century by the growth of a small number of soft drink manufacturers to national concerns, and as a consequence of this many small aerated drinks factories had to close, including those in Weston. In consequence there is little evidence of this industry in the present Weston townscape, but the same cannot be said of another past industry, the iron foundry of William Hillman. Little is known of the history of this firm, except that the business in Gloucester Road was probably founded by H. Pond, a Weston carrier, in about 1840, and taken over by Hillman in 1850. The firm continued to operate on the same site until the death of William Hillman's great-grandson W. A. Hillman in 1963. The various products of the foundry during its operation, ranging from drain covers to fencing, can still be found in the streets of Weston, bearing the maker's name.

The 20th century has seen a change in Weston's industrial structure with the growth of a much more varied manufacturing base. In fact little new industry came into the resort until the Second World War, the sole exception being Fussell's at Worle. Herbert James Fussell founded the rubber company which bears his name at Bath in 1920, but after a fire there, the operation was moved to the old gasworks site at Station Road, Worle. At their now much expanded 'Knightstone Mill', within which the old retort house of the gasworks survives, Fussell's are still producing and nationally distributing rubber products for the footware industry.

During the Second World War, sections of the aircraft industry were developed around Weston airport, and these provided the factory space in which more permanent peace-time activities could develop. Thus by 1951 some 15 major industries could be identified ranging from large-scale automobile reconditioning by Messrs Henley's, through book binding, the manufacture of prefabricated buildings (by the Bristol Aeroplane Company) to the sheet metal works of Andrews Brothers, who produced stainless steel kitchen equipment. In 1953 the *Bristol Evening Post* was able to report that because of the war-time influx of industry the employment situation had been well maintained, and that since then nine new employers had provided 2,700 new jobs. However, much of this activity had been directed to Weston by the Ministry of Supply in order to make use of the available factory space, and some activities, especially the making of prefabricated buildings, were only to be short-term employers. Indeed one enterprise, Andrews Brothers, was later to move to Birmingham.

Thus in the mid-1950s the employment situation in Weston, where the seasonal nature of the holiday trades always led to high winter unemployment, looked bleak. Fortunately both public and private enterprise intervened, and the outlook improved. In 1956 the operations of BAC Helicopters Ltd, were transferred to Weston, making use of the buildings originally designed to produce Bristol Beaufighters during the war, and used from 1945 to 1954 for the manufacture of BAC's range of prefabricated buildings. The helicopter concern was acquired by the Yeovil based firm of Westlands in 1961, and their Weston operation today concentrates on the repair of helicopters and the production of spare parts. In 1957 three former executives of the Bristol Aeroplane Company, Messrs H. J. Rush, E. J. Mills and S. C. Barge, set up a small firm to manufacture aluminium window frames. Their company, Alumin, expanded rapidly and in 1960 had 100 employees. Just ten years later, following its acquisition by Gardiners, Alumin had become the United Kingdom's largest manufacturer and exporter of aluminium windows, and had diversified into several other aspects of production and service for the building industry.

In 1958 two further events took place on the Weston industrial front. Firstly the Somerset shoe manufacturers C. & J. Clark Ltd. began the building of a factory on a site in Locking Road (the company already having a pilot plant in operation in warehouses in Whitecross Road), and secondly the Corporation made an overspill industry agreement with Birmingham. This agreement was made under the provisions of the 1952 Town Development Act, and it enabled the Corporation to set up an industrial estate to receive a limited amount of what was considered to be Birmingham's surplus industry. Despite some criticism a number of firms were attracted, and Weston proved to be a popular choice with Birmingham's workers. For example the firm of Compression Joints Ltd decided to move some of their operations to Weston, opening their factory at Oldmixon on 15 October 1963: about 1,000 of their Birmingham employees had applied for the 200 available jobs at the seaside. By 1973 the Corporation's Oldmixon estate had 14 companies employing some 1,500 people, and products ranged from fans and blowers to laboratory equipment and coin operated amusement machines. Since then further growth has occurred, and although the old problem of seasonal unemployment has not been eradicated, the possibility of more secure employment for many Westonians has been greatly increased.

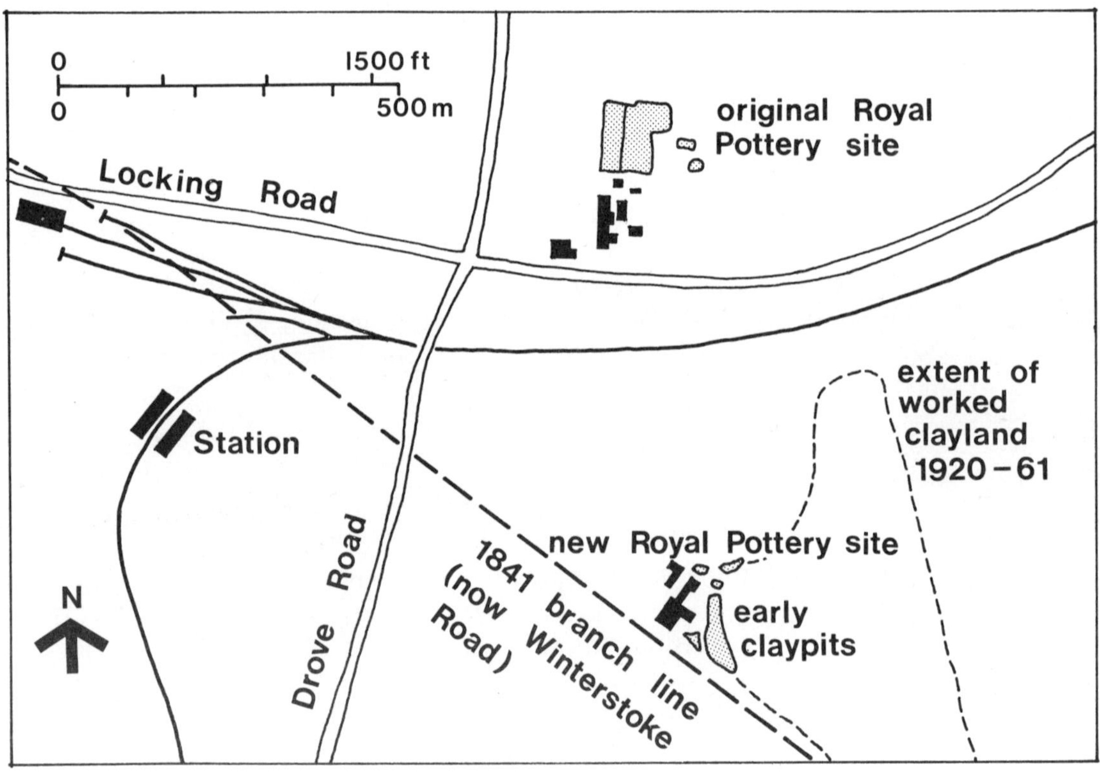

The sites of the Royal Potteries.

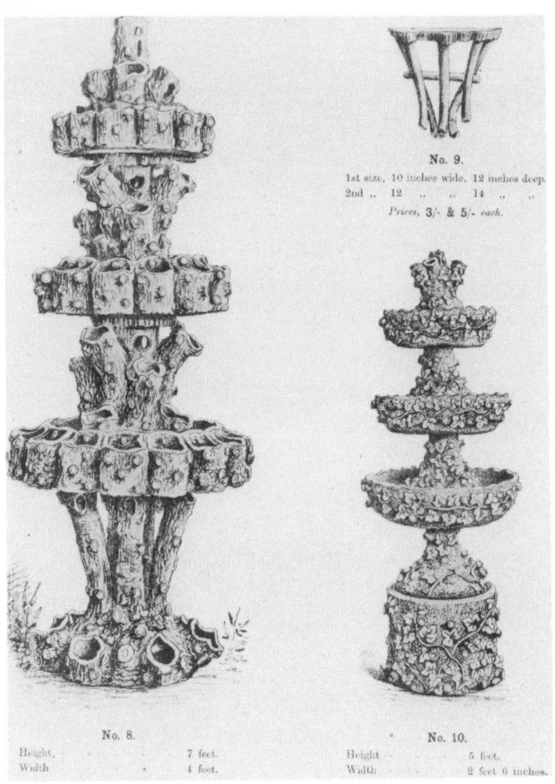

ABOVE: Royal Potteries, Locking Road works 1880's, LEFT: from the catalogue of about 1882, and RIGHT: Conway G. Warne, owner of the Potteries.

SHOWROOM
CONWAY G. WARN

LEFT: Royal Potteries Winterstoke site, c 1930; BELOW: the Potteries, CENTRE: one of the products — a brick. (WM) RIGHT: 'Mercury John' — 'Dr' John Bromfield.

ABOVE: Severn Road in the early 1900's and BELOW: Tremlett's Forge, Union Street.

ABOVE: Lance and Lance, High Street and BELOW: the results of the bombing of June 1942.

ABOVE: Warrilow and Co's garage in Oxford Street and BELOW: unloading coal at Knightstone Harbour.

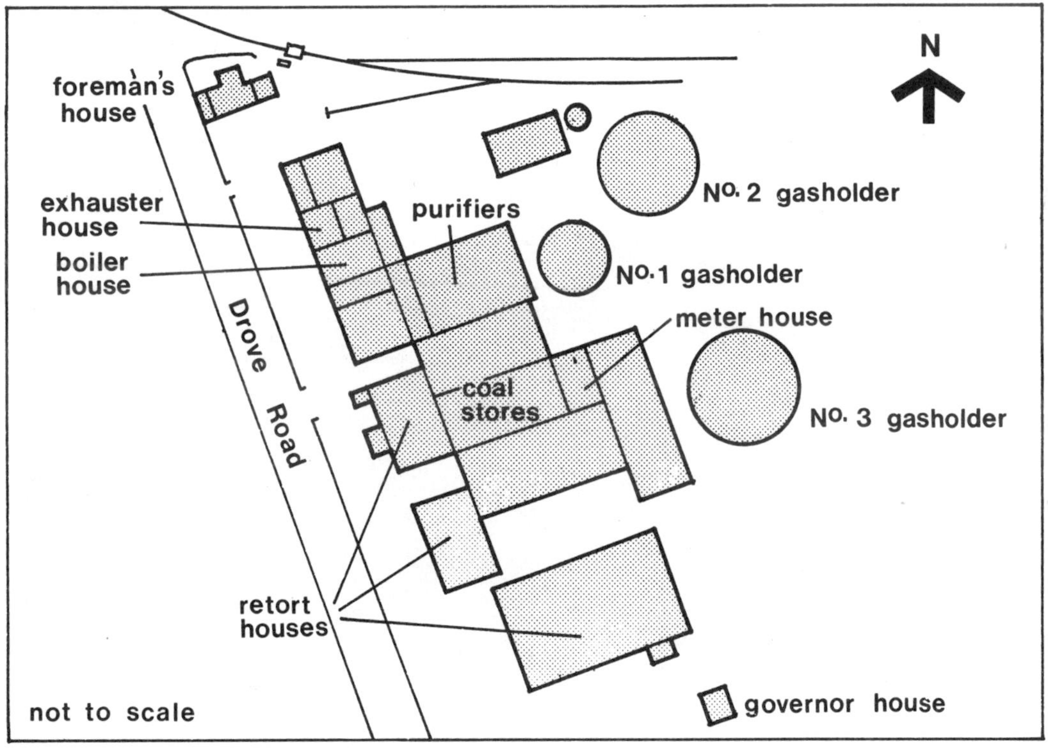

ABOVE: Meadow Street in 1911 and BELOW: Weston gasworks in 1914.

WESTON-SUPER-MARE

WAR BONDS COMMITTEE.

Business Men's Week,

March 4th to 9th.

WANTED!

24 AEROPLANES

The Chancellor of the Exchequer asks Weston to provide the value of 24 Aeroplanes (£60,000), as the Town's contribution to the mighty effort which the whole Nation is called upon to make this week.

Buy War Bonds

AND

War Savings Certificates.

Dropped from Aeroplane March 7, 1918

ABOVE: High Street in the 1930's, BELOW: A Spitfire raised with cash from INSET: the local appeal to raise funds for 24 planes in World War II.

The Common Weal

Throughout Weston's history as a resort much emphasis has been placed on the well-being of the visitors, and this care has endowed the town with many facilities which can also be enjoyed by the residents, except perhaps for those few crowded weeks at the height of the summer season. In addition, as its own population rose, the need for the education and entertainment of native Westonians was not forgotten.

Early Weston's growth was based partly on its reputation as a health resort, and as in many other places an attempt was soon made to establish a Sea Bathing Infirmary, on lines similar to the successful one in Margate. The driving force for this was the Bishop of Bath and Wells, who chaired an inaugural meeting at Wells on 29 March 1826. The purpose of his committee was 'to take into consideration the best method of establishing a Sea Bathing Infirmary on the coast of Uphill or Weston-super-Mare, for affording relief to diseased objects of charity'. The cause drew wide and influential support, subscribers including William Waldegrave, Hannah More and Dr E. L. Fox, as well as the Bishop as Chairman and J. H. Smyth-Pigott as Vice-Chairman. Enough money was available to enable a small start to be made and the 'Somerset Sea Bathing Infirmary' was ready to accept five patients by the end of the year. Whether or not any patients ever came to the Infirmary it is impossible to say, for there is no further record of its existence, nor even of its location.

The town remained without any sort of hospital facilities for many years, relying entirely upon its individual doctors until the opening of a public dispensary in 1857. In the same year the charitable Weston-super-Mare Lying-in Society was founded, and £54 was subscribed during its first year of existence, enough to aid '80 poor women' as well as supplying 4 boxes of clothes for loan. The present Queen Alexandra Memorial Hospital has its origins in 1865, although the original building was considerably extended during the remainder of the century by its first architect Hans Price. The present Boulevard frontage was added during the 1920s. The development of the hospital owed much to E. E. Baker and Henry Butt, who are commemorated by twin plaques beside the Boulevard entrance. The Royal Hospital, situated at the southern end of the esplanade, began life in 1868 as the Royal West of England Sanatorium, and is still referred to as 'The Sanatorium'. This replaced a temporary Sanatorium which had lately been established at Carlton

House with just four beds. Although it began in a small way, with just 30 beds on the Uphill Road site, the Royal Hospital soon expanded to take patients from all parts of the West of England. With various additions, including heated sea water baths built in 1890, it was treating over 3,000 patients annually in the 1920s.

A great variety of other additions were made to the resort during the 19th century, including the Kewstoke Toll Road, opened in 1848, Turkish Baths (1861), and several large hotels including the Grand Atlantic of 1888, which was an enlargement of an earlier building which had been used as a school. Visitors were also able to read the two local newspapers, the *Westonian,* which later became the *Mercury,* which had been started by James Dare in 1843, and the *Gazette,* first published in 1845 by Joseph Whereat. Both newspapers paid special attention to the needs of visitors, and followed the older spa tradition of printing a weekly list of resident visitors. The town was able to support those two weekly publications until the *Gazette* was absorbed by the *Mercury* in 1951. In 1855 the walks on Worlebury were opened to the public, while in 1892 the first golf course was laid out by the Weston-super-Mare Golf Club on land near Moorland Road, and in 1900 the Library and Museum building in the Boulevard was complete.

Following the First World War many more attractions were built, reflecting the confident spirit of the town. First came the Glentworth Bay enclosure scheme, which had for many decades been frustrated by financial restrictions. Opened in 1928 this was an instant success, and was used by over a quarter of a million people during 1929, although its range of facilities was incomplete until the reconstruction of the Rozel Bandstand in 1937. Also during the 1920s work began on the new Winter Gardens and Pavilion, for which the entire land purchase and legal costs were given to Weston by Henry Butt. The Pavilion and Gardens were completed in 1927 and cost £53,000. Finally, in 1937 Weston was granted Borough status, and as if to mark the occasion yet another large-scale municipal project came to fruition. This was the Pool, a large swimming pool complex, which was the first major amenity for the visitors to be located outside the Regent Street—Anchor Head area. The Pool, with its impressive 30 metre diving stage, attracted 109,000 bathers and 156,000 spectators in 1937, and remains one of Weston's major holiday facilities today.

Private investment has also contributed to visitor amenity during the present century, and perhaps the most important were the cinemas, of which Weston gained its fair share during the years of the celluloid boom. Moving pictures came to the town on a permanent basis in 1911 with the opening of the Electric Cinema, and some films were also shown in the Knightstone Pavilion during that year. The Regent, (later the Gaumont) in Regent Street followed in 1913, and the Central in Oxford Street in 1921. Then in 1928 the Palace Theatre, at the entrance to the site of the original Winter Gardens in the Boulevard, was converted for films, becoming the Tivoli Cinema. Finally in 1935 came the crowning glory of Weston's cinema history with the completion of the Odeon, designed by Cecil Howitt. Converted to a multi-screen theatre this fine example of 'odeon modern' architecture is now the only cinema in Weston, although the Gaumont survives as a bingo club.

Apart from the cinema the town also provides two theatres. The older, the Knightstone, opened in 1902 and has over the years seen a variety of entertainment from Dame Clara Butt to the circus, while for a time during the Second World War it was also used as a battledress factory. The running of the theatre was eventually taken over by Weston-super-Mare Corporation in 1957, and is now only opened for the summer season. The present splendid Playhouse Theatre, also municipally owned, was built to replace the original theatre on the site which burnt down in 1964. The first Playhouse was in fact a conversion made in 1946 of the former Market Hall, paid for with compensation money for the Grove Park Pavilion, which stood at the entrance to the park, and which had been bombed during the war.

Also popular in the town were concerts given by the famous Moggs band. This was founded in 1887 by Henry Mogg, a self-taught musician who had previously been a postman, and experienced not only great local popularity, but at its height in 1912 won the National Reed Band championship at Crystal Palace. Another of Weston's popular bands was the H. C. Burgess orchestra, which was formed in 1920 for the summer season. This soon became a permanent feature, and the orchestra performed regularly at the Rozel and the Winter Gardens until 1938. This form of entertainment is still popular with visitors and residents alike, and for the last 24 years Vernon Adcock and his orchestra have maintained the tradition at the Rozel and the Winter Gardens.

Interesting too, and an indication of changing tastes, are Weston's fish and chip shops. These mainly developed between the wars, but unlike most other forms of retailing at that time, were on the list of 'offensive trades', and thus subject to control by the Public Health Authority. It was through this control that fish and chip shops in the town centre became concentrated in St James Street, and had it not been for the licensing system far more would have been established both here and elsewhere in the town, many applications having been turned down. In 1922 there were just 4 licensed fish friers, in 1925 there were 5, rising to 6 in 1927, 7 in 1931, 9 in 1934 and finally 10 in 1935.

Neither have the needs of Weston's ordinary residents been forgotten, even to the extent of the opening of a charity soup kitchen in Little Orchard Street in 1862 to provide the poorest with some basic sustenance. Fortunately there seems to have been little really bad poverty in the town, and housing conditions and living standards were probably much better for the average Westonian than for many of the inhabitants of Victorian industrial cities. Thus the major area in which public facilities were needed was education, as few of the local working population were able to afford the fees of the numerous private schools which became established in the town.

Early in the 19th century a school and Sunday school for 100 children had been opened by Rev Stivard Jenkins, the curate of the parish church, but this does not appear to have survived for long. The first official Church School was St John's National Shool, which opened on a site in Church Road in 1845. The buildings were demolished in 1964 as part of the Technical College development. The British School (for the 'dissenting interest') opened in Hopkins Street in 1846, an infants' school at Christ Church in 1874, and the Walliscote Board Schools (designed by Hans Price) in 1897. Weston Grammar School began life in 1922 in Nithsdale Road, moving to its permanent building on the Uphill Castle field site only in 1935. Further education in Weston has its origins in the Working Men's Institute formed in 1858, and in 1859 the 'Albert Memorial Night School, Industrial Institution and Museum' had begun life in the Albert Hall behind Emmanuel Church. Later in the century proper provision for further education was made with the opening of the School of Science and Art in 1893. This is one of Hans Price's designs, and is still occupied by the Technical College's Art Department. Other schools have been built to serve the needs of a still growing town, together with the large new Technical College building, and Weston is now well provided with educational facilities.

National School, built 1846.

ABOVE: The College in 1871, now the Grand Atlantic Hotel and BELOW: the School of Science and Art opened in 1894.

ABOVE: Class 5, British School, Hopkins Street, 1895. CENTRE: Weston-super-Mare Swimming Club, 1890. BELOW: Moggs Band. In 1912 they won the Grand Challenge Shield in the National Reed Championships at Crystal Palace.

LEFT: Weston-super-Mare Town Band, 1908; RIGHT: Harry Mogg, founder of Moggs Band. BELOW: The Hospital, Alfred Street, built 1865.

ABOVE: Royal West of England Sanatorium, formerly Halfway House; CENTRE: the Sanatorium, now the Royal Hospital and BELOW: Walliscote Board School, opened 1897.

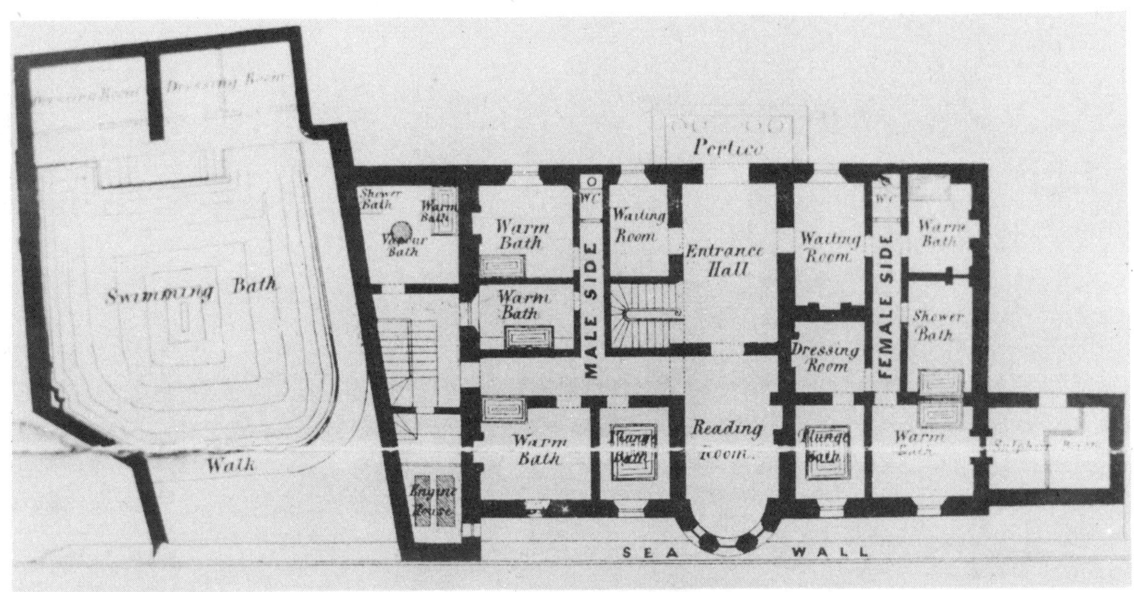

ABOVE: Knightstone Baths — the plan of 1860, and BELOW: opened in 1902.

LEFT: The proposed Opera House in Regent Street, 1900; RIGHT: Paul Radmilovic, winner of four Olympic Gold Medals for swimming, 1908-1920. BELOW: the great gale of 1903 left its mark on Knightstone Causeway.

ABOVE: The H. C. Burgess Orchestra and BELOW: different airs at Weston 'drome.

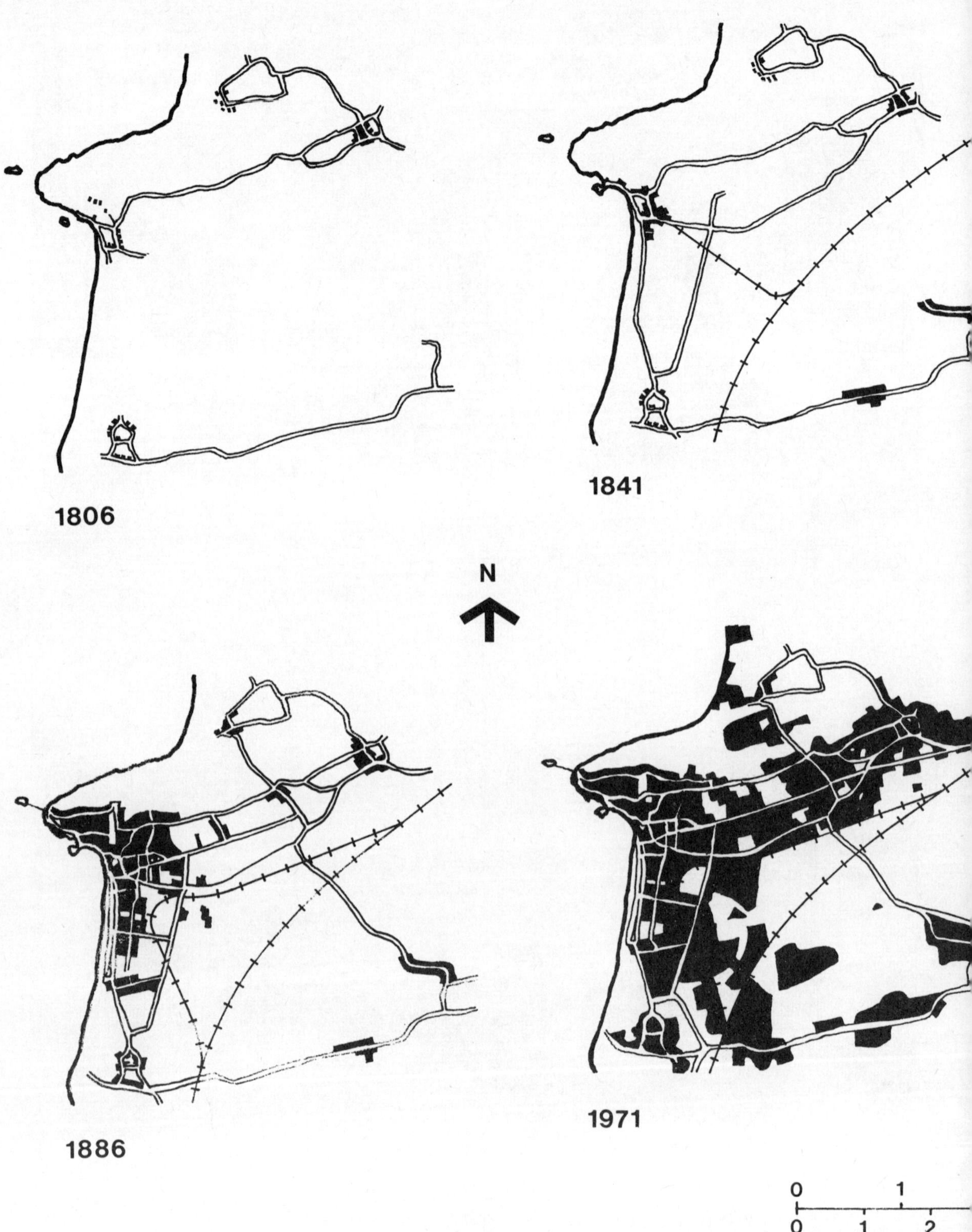
1806
1841
N
1886
1971
0
1
0
1
2

LEFT: The town's growth from 1806-1971, and RIGHT: some of the effects: ABOVE LEFT: the 19th century tradesmen and RIGHT: the enterprise of modern times, with BELOW: a modern disaster when fire hit the Playhouse Theatre in August 1964.

Weston's filmland: LEFT: the Electric Cinema, the town's first; RIGHT: the Tivoli, c 1935 and BELOW: the Odeon at that time.

Fair White City

Weston's history since 1800 has been one of growth and change, and of response to opportunity. The speculative building of the 19th century took various forms as it catered for a changing market, but it was always sympathetic to the local environment, using limestone from the town's own quarry on Worlebury, and local bricks from the Royal Potteries. Although this situation produced little individually outstanding architecture, the Victorian and Edwardian town was composed of many satisfactory groups of buildings, sensible layouts and attractive open spaces which were the result of careful planning and design. Also, the arm of local government, although not strong, was influential. The original Improvement Commissioners of 1842, through translations to Board of Health in 1859, Urban District Council in 1894 and Municipal Borough Corporation in 1937, had nearly always been favourable to 'improvement' in its widest sense, and had provided through its own actions some of the most important amenities. The Borough motto adopted in 1937 of 'Ever Forward' seemed singularly apt for an authority which had not only done so much for the holiday trades but had even been the first in Britain to build, at Milton Green, public housing under Addison's 1919 Housing Act, giving Weston the first modern council houses. More recently however the town has found itself at a crossroads, and in some important ways has been uncharacteristically backward at grasping opportunities.

At the heart of the dilemma is the fact that Weston has become more than just a seaside resort, although the holiday business remains vitally important. Firstly it has become the service centre for a considerable part of South Avon and North Somerset. Secondly it has developed new residential functions, both as a retirement area (a function of growing importance in most seaside resorts, often to the detriment of their social structure), and as a dormitory settlement for the Bristol industrial area. Thirdly, it has increased its own industrial employment in manufacturing, especially by the deliberate fostering of industrial estates and the overspill industry agreement with Birmingham.

It is mainly as a result of these three functions that Weston is experiencing rapid growth again today; indeed with the exception of the influx of evacuees in the Second World War the decade 1961-1971 saw the largest actual rise in Weston's population since the first census in 1801. In 1971 growth had in fact exceeded the limits of the old Municipal Borough, and the total population of the Weston urban area of that year was about 56,000. Planning Department estimates suggest that this figure may reach 76,000 by the mid-1980s and perhaps 100,000 by the end of the century. Although there is always some doubt as to the accuracy of the estimations, and it is worth noting that an earlier estimate in the 1958 *County Development Plan* suggested a 1971 population of 46,000, building during the 1970s has been extensive and growth is obvious to any traveller entering the town.

Weston can thus look forward to a period of continuing and substantial change which will bring many variations in its economy and social structure, and perhaps to a period of difficult adjustment to new circumstances. Much of the new development will, because of planning constraints and policy, be concentrated in the Worle area, close to the M5 junction, where low land makes for comparatively easy large scale building. Yet such development is often without character, and because of the standardisation of building materials and cost restrictions is unlikely to be sympathetic to the area. In addition, these large new developments, although at Worle possessing a 'District Centre', will still look to the old town centre for shopping, professional services and entertainment, while the presence of the beach and Weston's resort amenities are themselves a powerful attraction for newcomers.

Thus in both a practical and perhaps aesthetic sense the old limestone-built Victorian town is likely to remain as the essential spirit of Weston; it will be the area that marks Weston as an identifiable and special place for all its inhabitants, especially for the many new arrivals and their children. There can be little doubt from this viewpoint therefore that old Weston should be treated with the utmost care, for its character could be so easily changed by redevelopment unsympathetic to the surroundings. Neither would a careful conservation policy harm the tourist industry, for just as in the 19th century the needs of the visitor changed, so too have those of the 20th century tourist, who is fast learning to appreciate the cultural heritage left by the Victorians.

Some errors of judgement have undoubtedly been made, but fortunately a great deal of real interest and lasting value remains in Weston's historic core. What is needed for the remaining years of the century is something of the sensitivity and understanding of the earlier developers, who found ways in which to combine the creation of good environment with the ability to create wealth. New uses can be found for older buildings, good design can harmonise the new with the old, and there is little to be said for merely preserving the past for its own sake in a situation such as exists in Weston. It is only to be hoped that many of the new residents, along with established Westonians, will take an increasing interest in their town and its welfare, and ensure that at the beginning of the 21st century it will still be worthy of the title it earned at the beginning of the 20th as 'the fair white city by the Severn Sea'.

The many attractions of Weston, in this case amply displayed nearly seventy years ago.

Bibliography

Relatively few books have been written about the history of Weston-super-Mare, and in addition to those listed below readers are directed to the several archive sources within which are contained a vast and as yet relatively little explored wealth of information. Undoubtedly of greatest value are the files of the two local weekly newspapers, the many guide books and directories, deeds, official records, reports and pictures which are held in the Weston Central Reference Library and Woodspring Museum. The Somerset Record Office in Taunton also has extensive holdings relating to the town, and other holders of such records include Bristol Archives Office, Avon County Central Reference Library, Bristol and the library of Clevedon Court.

Atthill, R. *Mendip: A new Study*. David and Charles, 1976.

Bailey, Ronald *Weston-super-Mare: all you want to know and where you'll want to go: a souvenir handbook for visitors*. W. B. Frampton & Sons. 1955.

Baker, Ernest E. (Ed). *John Chilcotts' 1822 Guide to Weston-super-Mare*. Bristol, 1901 (Reprint with additions of 1822 edition).

Baker, Ernest E. *The Village of Weston-super-Mare. Historical Notes*. Weston-super-Mare, 1928.

Baker, Ernest E. *Weston-super-Mare Parish Church, 1226 to 1910*. Weston-super-Mare, 1910.

Brown, Bryan J. H. *Survey of the leisure industries of the Bristol region*. Unpublished PhD thesis, University of Bath, 1971.

Collinson, J. *The History and Antiquities of the County of Somerset*. 3 volumes, Bath, 1791. (*Index* volume, edited by F. W. Weaver and E. H. Bates, Taunton, 1898, and *supplement* by F. Madeline Ward, Taunton, 1939).

Farr, Grahame *Somerset harbours*. Johnson, 1954.

Gentry, P. W. *Tramways of the West of England*, Light Railway Transport League, 1960.

Harper, C. G. *The Somerset Coast*. Chapman and Hall, 1909.

Knight, F. A. *The Seaboard of Mendip*. Dent, 1902.

Little, Bryan. *Portrait of Somerset*. Hale, 4th ed. 1976.

MacInnes, C. M. and Whittard, W. F. (Eds). *Bristol and its adjoining Counties*. British Association for the adancement of Science, 1955. (Reprinted, E.P. 1973).

Maggs, Colin. *The Weston, Clevedon and Portishead Railway*. Oakwood Press, 1964.

Maggs, Colin. *The Weston-super-Mare Tramways*, Oakwood Press, 1974.

Mendip Society *Man and the Mendips*, 1971.

Palmer, W. R. *A Century of Weston-super-Mare History*. Bath, 1924.

Pawle, Gerald. *The Secret War*. Harrap 1956, reprinted 1972.

Rutter, J. *Delineations of the North Western Division of the County of Somerset*. Longman Rees & Co. 1829.

Rutter, J. *The Westonian Guide*. Longman Rees & Co. 1829.

Savage, R. J. G. (Ed). *Geological Excursions in the Bristol District*. University of Bristol, 1977.

Tomalin, David *Woodspring Priory*. Landmark Trust, 1974.

Weston-super-Mare History and Conservation Study Group. *Town Trails*, numbers 1-4. and *Occasional Papers* series.

Index

Numbers in *italics* refer to illustrations

Subscribers

Presentation copies

1 Weston-super-Mare Charter Trustees
2 Woodspring District Council
3 Avon County Council
4 Weston-super-Mare Library
5 Woodspring Museum
6 G. P. Rye, FLA

7 John Loosley ALA
8 Bryan Brown, BSc, PhD
9 Clive Birch
10 Kenneth John Coles
11 Albert Edward Worrall
12 Miss J. E. Saker
13 Zita Coorg
14 Dinah Hayes
15 J. Sanderson
16 John J. Brock
17 Mrs J. Sweet
18 P. J. Tottle
19 D. R. Curtis
20 D. S. Wicks
21 Margaret Higgison
22 J. O. Howden
23 E. J. Guthrie
24 Mrs J. Hall
25, 26 Miss J. M. Simmons
27 Mrs E. Day
28 A. F. Hutson
29 Mrs P. Matthews
30 Gerald Frederick Wadham
31 Brendon Cottrell
32 Mr & Mrs S. R. Taylor
33 Mrs K. M. Austin
34 Peter Heaton
35 W. Richard German
36 Peter Chard
37 Archie Wilkins
38 J. Ticehurst
39 Alan P. White & Angela K. White
40 A. J. M. Jeffery
41 Miss B. Findley
42 Mrs E. M. Faulkner
43 E. Sillifant
44 Nicholas John Corcos
45 Miss A. Watts
46 L. Trenchard
47 Alec S. Baxter
48 Doreen Phipps
49 W. R. Bowler
50 Margaret Ann Woolley
51 W. Pearce
52 D. H. Stabbins
53 C. D. Locke
54 L. V. Crews
55 D. C. Knox
56 B. S. James
57 T. M. B. Moody
58 Lucinda Dunstone
59 Olga J. Deam
60 Mrs Florence Mary Wilkinson
61 P. M. Guerin
62 S. D. Rendell
63 Geoffrey Parry Rye
64 Keith Refault
65 Philip W. Heeks
66 D. J. Dodgson
67 Mr & Mrs M. Foreman
68 Barbara Betty Hodder
69 Ann Margaret Walker
70 John P. C. Tarry
71 Mrs C. M. Walker
72 Mrs J. M. Moody
73 Mrs M. Dougherty
74 T. V. T. Garlick
75 R. E. V. Smith
76 Mr & Mrs D. M. McCutcheon
77 Richard Graves
78 Mrs H. E. Stevenson
79 William Henry Purnell
80 Miss M. J. Walker
81 Howard Smith
82 J. N. Todd
83 H. E. G. Gooding
84 Broadoak School
85 S. J. Hartree
86 Joy Carter
87 Martha Perriam
88, 89 Mrs K. Cross
90 Mary Allen Ball
91 Mrs Helen Buell
92 Mrs J. Pitcairn
93 E. M. May
94 William Stanley Green
95 Mrs E. M. Mace
96 Martin Taylor
97 G. A. Wellum
98 Mrs B. David
99 Mrs S. Mackay
100 Mrs D. A. Edwards
101 Mrs J. Lee
102 R. M. E. Lees
103 David Gwyn Cook
104 W. Ainsworth
105 Dr Joseph A. Farley
106 Mrs C. Hodnett
107 E. G. Wirth
108 Miss R. Martyn
109 Valerie Clout
110 David D. Sutton
111 A. J. Page
112 G. D. Holburd
113 Mrs M. Martin
114 May Green
115 Philip Roger Caulfield Day
116 Cyril Henry Savill
117 R. H. Channing
118 Mr & Mrs R. Long
119 N. A. Newnham
120 Joyce White
121 J. G. Roberts
122 Malcolm Timmis
123 Mr & Mrs W. Norman Beese
124 K. F. Watts
125 B. A. Lammas
126 Miss B. M. Withers
127 William John Hayden
128 D. Day
129 Mrs J. H. Addison
130 Mrs E. E. Eyre
131 Kevin Speakman
132 Brian Williams
133, 134 T. Gilbert
135 L. Ward
136 R. E. Tuck
137 Mrs Maria Harrison
138 L. R. Chappell
139 Mrs C. M. Jones
140 Mrs E. T. Clutterbuck
141 J. C. Sutton
142 M. E. Bunston
143 G. J. Reynolds
144 Stephen D. Rigby
145 Keith Edmond Monk
146 L. N. Price
147 J. F. Barnan
148 Mrs I. M. Court
149 Charles Robert Smart
150 Harry Galloway
151 Mrs S. E. Redman
152 M.E. White AIB
153 Mrs S. M. A. Cox
154 C. Charsley
155 Frances Amanda Johns
156 I. Ruth Price
157 Mrs I. Godbeer
158 George D. Forbes
159 Captain P. J. Parrott
160 Cheryl Robinson
161 Mrs K. Neville
162 Irene C. Jones
163 J. G. Crowe
164 S. H. Webber
165 B. M. Ridge

166 Joyce Wilmott
167 Mrs E. Wagstaff
168 Miss J. S. Wiles
169 Miss A. M. Griffin
170 Mrs E. D. Westlake
171 S. Dolman
172 Paul Martin Blockside
173 Clive Garth Wall
174 Lynne Bryce
175 A. J. Norman
176 Donald Albert Hunt
177 Simon Hughs
178 Frederick Arnold Downes
179 Gordon Trevor Pratt
180 Leslie George Miles
181 John Mason
182 Pam Cattell
183 S. T. Gardiner
184 Brenda Rigby
185 Edward Mayhew
186 Terence Victor Clapp
187 Mrs E. Black
188 Peter J. Stephen
189 Charles P. Oxley
190 Ann Holding
191 W. G. Smith
192 A. M. J. Eddy
193 M. W. Southcombe
194 Henry C. Marsh
195 Robert Wilson Cross
196 John R. Andow
197 W. H. Willis
198 Donald Sage Sutherland
199 N. Shaw
200 Roy James Dare
201 Mrs J. Tucker
202 Mrs A. Leeworthy
203 Mr & Mrs J. R. Blizzard
204 Mrs J. Wilson
205 Miss P. Ricardo
206 Miss S. Ricardo
207 J. Rubery
208 J. White
209 H. L. Lethersby
210 S. G. Hewitt
211 Mrs M. Kingswell
212 W. A. G. Baker
213 Geoffrey Ruston Simmons
214 D. H. C. Norman
215 Eric James
216 Mrs Arthur
217 J. B. Ullyott
218 Stanley Noel Brookes
219 Doreen F. Day
220 Donald Bulmer
221 Mrs J. M. Cripps
222 Miss A. M. Moss
223 J. M. Sperring
224 David A. Dennis
225 James C. Kyte
226 Mrs L. Hunt
227 K. Ewart-Clarke
228 L. Mealand
229 Robert Quinlan
230 M. A. Hitchins
231 John Crockford-Hawley
232 Derek Michael Saville
233 S. H. Jones
234 J. D. Headford
235 I. H. Hillier
236 Miss P. E. Hubbard
237 Thomas Hodgkiss
238 Lily Marguerite Deacon
239 Mrs E. L. Thurlow
240 Mrs W. Bazeley
241 N. P. Jenkins
242 P. L. Chaplin
243 S. G. Carter
244 Dennis A. Newnam
245 Barry Stringer
246 Maureen Price
247 Mrs R. Pollock
248 Richard Bowen
249 Paul White
250 Jeremy J. Herring
251 Judith Heyman
252 Mrs R. E. M. Hayward
253 Jack Donkin
254 David Oldroyd
255 Vince Russett
256 Stanley Terrell
257 Mrs S. Ryall
258 R. H. Mosely
259 B. H. Coggan
260 Mr & Mrs R. Cox
261 J. A. Cox
262 Mrs J. Leppard
263 Mrs S. E. Kerk
264 Paul David Knight
265 Mrs H. Astill
266 Mrs P. A. Marsh
267 Jane Elizabeth Roseff
268 Daphne Mason
269 Nigel Evans
270 Christopher Potts
271 Nora Chackett
272 David Driver
273 Mark Furlong
274 Mrs S. Gribble
275 James F. Hinett
276 Ian A. R. Vowles
277 Robert Perkins
278 Margaret Jennifer Rowland
279 Mrs Joy Markham
280 D. M. Hobbs
281 Mr & Mrs J. J. Frankpitt
282 Mrs M. E. Frankpitt
283 Harry W. King
284 B. J. Gosling
285 Mrs C. M. James
286 Graham Thomas Sanders
287 Sandra Marsh
288 A. C. Jacobs
289 Michael Usher
290 A. Seaney
291 Mrs Jill Banwell
292 Weston-super-Mare
293 Technical College
294 Carol Powlesland
295 Miss C. Rolph
296 Mrs J. Merrett
297 John C. Moon
298 Anita E. Foord
299 Miss I. M. James
300 Mr & Mrs W. C. Loosley
301 C. W. Wilcox
302 B. Maurice
03 H. G. Williams
304 J. Saker
305 Mrs M. F. Whitham
306 Kim Amesbury
307 Woodspring Central Library
308 Dorothy Bingham-Hall
309 George Hather
310 Mr & Mrs Dennis Reynolds
311 K. A. Poole
312 Philip & Mary Ashley
313 T. Dedges
314 Miss J. N. Hall
315 A. J. Clements
316 D. G. Morgan
317 Mr & Mrs D. Tabrett
318 Miss T. R. Keen
319 Mrs E. M. Yates
320 S. R. Lyons
321 Frank Farley
322 Marks and Spencer Ltd
323 J. P. Hall
324 J. W. B. McKenna
325 Dorothy Salvage
326 Miss K. A. Player
327 Mrs M. M. Ray
328 Albert E. C. Lee
329 Arthur Lamb
330 Miss O. L. I. Morgan
331-334 Sterling Books
335 D. C. Whimster JP, MA
336 David J. Gay
337 Mrs M. Southern
338 Edgar Topham
339 Eileen Wreford
340 Mrs E. James
341 John Leonard Pope
342 Mrs B. Frost
343 Pamela Hodder
344 Kenneth Fowkes
345 Mr & Mrs G. Dickason
346 Mr & Mrs Gordon W. Couch
347 Maurice H. Exton
348 Frank Watts
349 Weston Teachers'
350 Centre
351 Wyvern School
352 Library
353 Corpus Christi School
354 Dr M. G. Hinton
355 Edwina Brafield
356 Somerset County Council
357-364 Somerset County Library
365 Somerset Record Office
366-414 Avon County Library
415 Marjorie Plummer
416 W. N. Tinsley
417 Stephen & Vicki Wegg-Prosser
418 Malcolm & David Read
419 Joan & Tony Lammiman
420 Beaver Reprographics Ltd
421 Victoria & Albert Museum
422 H. L. Coggins
423 Mr & Mrs A. Coggins
424 G. B. Atkinson
425 Mrs Alys Nuttall
426 C. P. Cammack
427 C. H. Brown
428 Mrs D. J. Haskins
429 Marjorie Joyce Bizley
430 B. Doorbar
431 Miss G. Moore
432 Mr & Mrs I. M. Norman
433 William Soper
434 J. A. Morgan
435 Charles Skilton
436 Mrs F. Fitzgerald
437 Mrs B. Smith
438 Mrs Stella Hill
439-442 Dr Bryan Brown
443 Peter Loosley
444 Helen Loosley
445 Daniel Loosley
446 Elizabeth Collard
447 Barbara June Down & Julie Ann Down
448 S. A. Hedges
449 Colin R. McArthur
450 F. G. Manning
451 Eric Wilkinson
452 A. H. Andrews

Remaining names unlisted.

ENDPAPERS FRONT: Weston from Knightstone in 1858.

BACK: Weston from above, 1978. (WAP)